MW01489570

RACHEL JOY SCOTT
Her Life and Legacy

By: Darrell and Sandy Scott

Joy Concepts
©2024

For other books by Darrell Scott go to:
Amazon: Books by Darrell Scott

For video poems and vlogs by Darrell Scott
Go to YouTube: Awareness by Darrell Scott

To have Darrell Scott speak in your church,
business, or community event contact:
Dana: gocardinals2009@gmail.com
or
Peter: peterdeanello@mac.com

RACHEL JOY SCOTT
1981-1999

Dedicated to the memory of my daughter, who
was killed in the 1999 massacre at Columbine
High School. Her life and legacy continues to
touch millions of people around the world

CHAPTERS

FORWARD

By: Kayleigh McKenany

(Former White House Press Secretary & Television Commentator)

I stared at the television in complete bewilderment, trying to comprehend the harrowing images playing before my 11-year-old eyes. Police swarming a brick school building. Children walking out with their hands above their heads. Tears, embraces, and human sadness on full display. These were the images of Columbine High School on April 20, 1999, the tragic day when 13 innocents lost their lives.

The shooting at Columbine High School rocked the nation to its core. It was an unforgettable tragedy for a young generation that watched evil play out before its very eyes. But in the days that followed, we would learn about the courage, faith, and heart of a young girl whose testimony would change so many lives, including my own.

17-year-old Rachel Joy Scott was eating her lunch outside when a cascade of bullets struck her and her friend. One of the two shooters approached Rachel and asked her a question: "Do you still believe in God?" to which she replied, "You know I do!" Rachel professed her faith boldly and confidently, and she lost her life moments later.

As a sixth-grade girl, I was awe-struck by Rachel's bravery and her unwavering faith. Days after Columbine, I watched Rachel's funeral on television, her white casket adorned with signatures from family and friends.

The testimonies of her friends told the story of a girl whose animating principle was love. One teenage boy tearfully recounted his memory of Rachel: "All my life I prayed that someone would love me and make me feel wanted. God sent me an angel." His story was just one of many.

5

Rachel befriended the homeless, the bullied, the outcast. Millions of people worldwide watched Rachel's memorial service, and in doing so, heard the message that her life portrayed of kindness and love. Rachel's memorial, however, was not the end of the story – it was just the beginning.

One year after Rachel's death, Rachel's father, Darrell Scott, and mother, Beth Nimmo, published *Rachel's Tears*. The book contained pages from Rachel's personal journals – her drawings, poems, and musings about the world.

I eagerly consumed every page of the book. Rachel's journal entries displayed an uncanny amount of wisdom for a teenager. Her heart and compassion for others reverberated off the pages. As a middle school girl myself, I found her writings to be real and relatable concerning the struggles we all face growing up.

Most of all, I was astounded by what Darrell describes as Rachel's "strong prophetic sense of her purpose on this planet." In one drawing Rachel traced her hand and wrote, "These hands belong to Rachel Joy Scott and will someday touch millions of people's hearts." Her final words to her teacher on the day of the shooting echoed that. "I'm going to have an impact on the world," Rachel told her teacher just before she lost her life.

Not only did Rachel appear to know that she would touch the world, she also had what I would describe as a premonition of her death. In a drawing of her hand, Rachel penned these words around the perimeter of the page: "He gave his life for me - - I will give my life to him." Amazingly, 11 months before her passing, she wrote the most direct indication about her future: "This will be my last year Lord. I have gotten what I can. Thank you." Wow! And in yet another part of her journal, she even asserted that she would die by homicide.

I was stunned by Rachel's writings, walking away with the distinct feeling that Rachel was an angel on earth. So inspired by her testimony, I did school projects on Rachel's life and shared her story with many.

I even began writing my own journals to God, spending many nights of my youth writing out prayers to God in the tradition of Rachel's journals.

Later in life, when I wrote my first book, I knew that I wanted to dedicate it to my hero, Rachel Joy Scott. I reached out to Rachel's Challenge, an organization created in her name designed to prevent school violence. Through Rachel's Challenge, over 30 million people have heard her story, and the results speak for themselves. Rachel's message of compassion has averted several school shootings and more than 150 suicides each year.

In reaching out to Rachel's Challenge, I hoped to inform Rachel's father, Darrell, about my book dedication. Within a day, I connected with Darrell, and I had the distinct honor of sharing the impact that his daughter had on my life.

As I wrote previously in *The New American Revolution*, "I will never forget taking in those horrific images [of Columbine] as a young 11-year-old girl. It was the day that I saw evil and realized that it was alive in this world. On April 20, 1999... evil was at work, but it could not extinguish the good." Rachel's life embodied that good, and no amount of darkness could cover her bright light – a light that shines just as brightly today as Rachel's story continues to transform hearts.

Rachel's life lit a fire within me, hemming my Christian faith even more deeply into my soul. I have no doubt that Rachel's life testament, as expressed in the pages that follow, will change your life too. Through Rachel's journals, I came to know her as a friend, and it is my prayer that when I leave this earth, Rachel will be there to meet me.

Kayleigh McEnany

PREFACE

Many books have been written about Columbine and quite a few about Rachel Joy Scott. So, why another book? Because this book provides a fuller, uncensored view of Rachel and her diaries.

In it you will find stories of her legacy in the decades following her death that are not found in any other writings. It is written through the eyes of her dad, Darrell, and her stepmom, Sandy. Although the book is authored by both Darrell and Sandy Scott, it is written in the first person from the viewpoint of Darrell.

Darrell and Sandy Scott are the founders of _Rachel's Challenge_, a K-12 public school assembly and training program that has become one of the largest of its kind in the world. It has inspired and trained over 35 million students in live settings in the two and a half decades after Rachel's death, with millions more to be impacted.

This book is not associated with, published by, nor sold through _Rachel's Challenge_. It has both spiritual, scriptural, and religious content that is reflected through Rachel's life and writings that are never used in public school programs of _Rachel's Challenge_.

The authors have abided by the restrictions and guidelines of public education and long ago do not include any religious content in the school program, _Rachel's Challenge_. This book will not be referred to; it will not be sold; nor will it be promoted in public school events or any educational conferences. It is strictly being made available to the public who want to know more about Rachel Scott's life, writings, and legacy.

Rachel was kind, deeply compassionate, and had a strong desire to serve God with all her heart, but she was not perfect. She struggled with things that she wrote about in her diaries, and she, like most teenagers, did things that she knew were wrong.

But no one who knew Rachel, or even read her writings, could ever doubt her love for God and others. Like Jesus, she was known to be a "friend of sinners." Jesus got along much better with prostitutes, winos, and bartenders than he did with the religious, self-righteous pharisees. So, before you judge my daughter - - take a look at Jesus - - and then take a look at yourself.

Jesus himself said: *"The son of man came eating and drinking, and they say, 'Here is a glutton, a drunkard, a friend of tax collectors and sinners.' But wisdom is proved right by her deeds."* (Matt. 11:19 NIV). Rachel's deeds, drawings, and dialect from her diaries are her proof.

Throughout this book you will find **QR** codes attached to the text. They will give you a much deeper view, through videos, of Rachel's life. Rachel - - we love you! *Dad and Sandy*

Chapter 1
A DAY OF TERROR AND DEATH

Police dispatcher: *"Jefferson County 911."*

Patti Neilson: *"Yes, I am a teacher at Columbine High School. There is a student here with a gun!"*

Dispatcher: *"Has anybody been injured ma'am?"*

Patti: *"Yes - - yes, and the school is in a panic! And I'm in the library and I've got students - -* (she screams) *Under the table kids! Heads under the table!"*

Those were the first moments that the outside world would begin to realize that something unprecedented was happening at a public high school in Littleton, Colorado.

Bang! Bang! Boom! The echoing sounds of gunfire and exploding pipe bombs could be heard in the halls of Columbine High School for the next terrifying half hour.

Two boys draped in long dark overcoats carrying shotguns, pistols, and pipe bombs slipped into the back of the school after having shot several students on the lawn outside.

For over a year, Eric Harris and Dylan Klebold had been scheming and planning for this very moment. They had written out their horrific plans in their journals and even made videos depicting what would happen on that fateful day.

They had originally chosen April 19 because it was the anniversary of the Oklahoma City bombing which killed 168 innocent victims, including many babies and small children.

10

Instead, as admirers of Adolph Hitler, they brought their destruction on Hitler's 110th birthday, April 20, 1999.

Their plan was to plant two 20-pound propane tanks, attached to a timer, in the cafeteria at lunch time when it would be crowded.

They stealthily snuck the tanks into the cafeteria, set the timer, and covered it with a couple of coats. They then went back to their cars to wait for the explosion, where they had guns that they planned to use to pick off the survivors after the blast. Fortunately, the timer never went off. Unfortunately, the shooting was about to begin.

Investigators reported that if those tanks had exploded, over 500 people would have died that day.

Disappointed with their initial failure, the two boys got out of their cars and headed for the back of the school. They wore long coats to conceal the pipe bombs and guns underneath. A teacher and 12 students would lose their lives that day.

My daughter, Rachel, my son, Craig, my niece, Sarah, and my nephew, Jeff, were all there at the school.

After talking with Patti, the dispatcher relayed this information to police units: *"Attention south units, have possible shots fired at Columbine High School, 6201 South Pierce, possibly in the south lower lot toward the east end. One female is down."*

That female was my daughter, Rachel.

THE FIRST THREE ROSES

Rachel Joy Scott sat in Mrs. Sue Caruther's English class at Columbine High School drawing a picture. The date was April 20, 1999. The time was 10:58 a.m. She had started her drawing earlier, in her math class, and was now putting on the finishing touches. She was carefully sketching out a picture of a rose in her diary. She had drawn this same rose on previous occasions.

1ST ROSE

The first one she drew months earlier, is what I would interpret as "The Birth of the Rose." It looks as though it is emerging out of a womb, shaped like a heart. The womb is not only heart-shaped, but it also looks like pieces of a puzzle - - - indicating an element of mystery.

The "baby" rose has a line spiraling upward around it, symbolic of her human spirit, as though it is destined to ascend. There were lots of spirals in her artwork.

RACHEL'S DRAWING THE BIRTH OF A ROSE

The spiral is an inspirational symbol that represents transcendence from an earthly, or natural realm to a spiritual dimension. Both the words, "spiral" and "inspiration" have the root word "spirit" in them. *Inspire means "in spirit."* Inspiration can come from a book, a movie, a song, a poem, artwork, etc. Not just scripture, sermons, or religion.

At the risk of sounding too mystical, I will tell you that Rachel's birth (*like the birth of the rose*) had elements of both inspiration and mystery as well. I already had two wonderful daughters, Bethanee, and Dana, and I was really hoping for a boy on the third round.

Back in those days, most parents did not have access to ultrasound imaging of their unborn son or daughter. However, there were several traditional indications of which sex the child would be: a son or a daughter. All the pregnancy symptoms were indicating that this child would be a boy. In fact, we already had a boy's name picked out and ready to go - - Craig.

Let me tell you how and why I picked that name.

I grew up in Shreveport, Louisiana and lived across the street from a very athletic kid by the name of Terry. He was a year older than me. Terry was good at every sport he played. Not just good - - he was outstanding! The only thing I could beat him at was ping pong. We played basketball in our driveway and football in his backyard.

In high school, Terry became the quarterback for our football team, the Woodlawn Knights. But he also was good at all the other sports, especially track. He was great at throwing the javelin.

One day in English class, I glanced out the window and was shocked to see Michael Landon, famous for tv roles in *Bonanza* and *Little House on the Prairie*, strolling down the sidewalk with Terry. Michael broke the world record in throwing the javelin in 1954.

Terry beat that record in 1966, and Michael came to meet Terry and congratulate him.

The Olympic committee wanted Terry to compete in the 1968 Olympic javelin competition, but he decided to save his arm for football. It was a wise decision - - because Terry would become the number one draft pick by the Pittsburgh Steelers in 1970 and go on to win 4 Super Bowls!

Yes - - Terry Bradshaw lived right across the street.

So, what does that have to do with the name, "Craig?" Well, Terry had a younger brother named Craig and I had a younger brother named Larry. Larry and Craig were best friends and Craig was always hanging out at our house. I liked his name, and decided that when I had a son, I would call him Craig.

But shortly before "Craig" arrived on this planet, we had a visiting minister staying in our home for a week. He was a very humble, spiritual man, by the name of Lattie McDonough.

The day before he left, he asked if he could say a blessing over the unborn child, and of course, we said, "Yes." That's when something rather strange happened.

14

Lattie knew how much I wanted a son, but as he began to pray, he stopped - - looked over at me - - and said, *"I want to say that this child is a boy, but I feel strongly that I can't say that. What I can say is that she will bring joy to the hearts of many people."*

When he spoke those words, I felt two things very distinctly - - and I never forgot them. The first was a feeling of disappointment that I might not get the son I wanted, and the second was that this would be *a very special daughter* - - which immediately erased my first feeling!

There was a sense of the prophetic element in Lattie's prayer, which turned out to be true. Because Lattie said that she would bring joy to many people, we chose that as her middle name - - Rachel <u>Joy</u> Scott! Seventeen years later we would have these words inscribed on her gravestone: *"She was the 'Joy' of our lives."*

Her life began with a blessing, proclaiming that she would bring joy to many hearts. In death, her gravestone would declare that she brought joy to our lives. But her legacy would prove, beyond a shadow of a doubt, that her story would bring both tears *and* joy to millions of people around the world.

Psalm 30:5 says, *"Weeping may endure for a night, but joy comes in the morning."* That verse would become a reality to our family, and to millions of others, in the years following Rachel's death.

Maybe I'm reading too much into that first drawing of "The Birth of a Rose" - - but then, maybe not. I'll leave that to your own opinion.

So, on August 5, 1981, Joy burst into this world! Rachel JOY Scott. Someone told me that her middle name was an acronym representing: **J**esus - - **O**thers - - **Y**ourself.

2ᴺᴰ ROSE

Now - - moving on to her second drawing of a rose. In this picture, the rose is fully mature, but it is not growing out of the ground. Instead, it is growing out of a Columbine flower.

The rose is America's national flower, and the Columbine is the Colorado state flower. So, she drew America's national flower emerging out of Colorado state's flower. You can also see a second Columbine flower on the left side of the picture. Just as there are two large Columbines, there are also two large crosses. The drawing seems to be connecting the Columbines and the crosses.

The rose has drops coming from an unknown source. The drops trickle down the spiral line, past the Columbine flower, and soak into the ground.

For years, I thought that those dark drops were blood drops - - but eventually I came to see them as something completely different. I'll tell you about that later.

Of course, the Columbine flower also represents Rachel's high school. The word, "Columbine", means "like a dove." This is the same description given for the Holy Spirit that descended on Jesus when he was baptized in the Jordan River. John the Baptist saw the heavens open and the Holy Spirit descending on Jesus like a dove.

There is one other item that I would like to mention, which is a small web up on the right side beside the rose. It has tiny crosses and Columbine flowers meshed in its strands.

I don't know what the web represents, but someone suggested that it might represent the internet, which was in its infant stage at the time. Perhaps Rachel sensed that her story, which embraced both Columbine and the cross, would be viewed by millions of people in years to come. *(Just a guess)*

The most prominent illustration in her drawing is the fish symbol in the center. Early Christians used the fish symbol to identify each other while keeping their identity hidden from the Roman government to avoid persecution.

The Greek word for 'fish' is 'ichthus' *(transliterated from the Greek)*. Early Christians formed an acrostic from these letters as follows: I= Iesous *(Jesus)*; CH=Christos *(Christ)*; TH=Theous *(God)*; U= UIOS *(Son)*; SOTER *(Savior)*. Therefore, the idea of the fish, or the sight of the symbol, would immediately identify one as a Christian.

Rachel's fish drawing is dissected by the largest of the crosses, where the words "Jesus Christ" are written, accompanied by two smaller crosses.

17

Inside the fish she wrote the verse from John 15:3, "*Greater love hath no man than this, that a man would lay down his life for his friends.*"

Many believe that the Romans killed Jesus (*the political system*). Others believe it was the religious Jews (*religious system*). And some say it was the diabolical plan of the devil. But Jesus said that only he had the power to lay down his own life.

As you will see in the coming chapters, Rachel seemed willing to do whatever it took to make a difference in this world - - including dying.

3rd ROSE

In her third rose, you can see a mixture of dark drops as well as clear drops that look like tears. However, you still can't see the source from which the drops are falling.

This third rose would be connected to her hand, which was covered with spirals (inspiration). She had drawn pictures of her hand on two other occasions. The first time was when she and my daughter, Dana, wrote some things on the back of Rachel's dresser. Rachel was 13 years old at the time.

Dana had forgotten all about that until 2 years after Rachel died when she was helping move Rachel's dresser from one room to another and discovered their writings from years earlier. It was Christmas Day, 2001 when Dana called me and said, *"Dad, you're not going to believe what we just found!"*

On the back of that dresser Rachel had written, *"These hands belong to Rachel Joy Scott and will someday touch millions of people's hearts."* See the QR code to learn more about this amazing story.

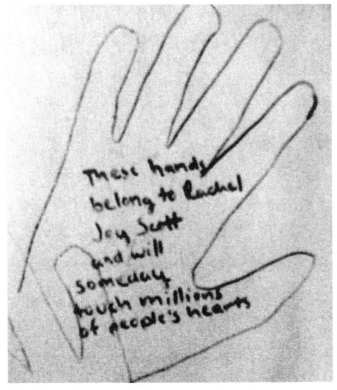

The second time she drew on outline of her hand was on a poster that she did for a school project. In today's cultural climate it would not be allowed, but it was back then.

Around the perimeter she wrote, *"He gave his life for me - - I will give my life to him."* In the center she made a powerful statement:

"Tomorrow is not a promise - - but a chance." As you can see, all 3 hand drawings had to do with a sense of destiny and purpose.

3 roses and 3 hands all connected by a symbol of the spirit - - the spiral. All prophetically pointing toward purpose and destiny. But what was the source of those drops that we saw on the roses?

Perhaps she answered that question for us in this drawing. The drops originated as tears following from her eyes before they turn dark when they encounter the flower below.

Now, let's get back to where we started - - the English class where Rachel was drawing her fourth and final rose. As she was putting the last touches on her picture, Mrs. Caruther's walked by and stopped at Rachel's desk. She looked over Rachel's shoulder at the drawing and cleared her throat. Perhaps Rachel thought she was about to be reprimanded.

But instead, Mrs. Caruthers told us later that she asked, *"Rachel, that is beautiful - - what does it mean?"* Rachel's didn't directly answer that question - - instead she said, *"Oh Mrs. Caruthers, it's not finished, but I'm going to have an impact on the world."*

In hindsight, Mrs. Caruthers was stunned, as we were, by Rachel's reply! To hear Mrs. Caruthers tell this story use the QR code:

At that moment the bell rang to end the class, releasing all the students to go to lunch. This 4th and final drawing of a rose *(you'll see it later)* would become a huge part of Rachel's legacy, and its story would be told to over 35 million people in live settings in the coming decades. This does not count the millions who would see it on television shows or read about it in books.

Her final words to Mrs. Caruthers on that fateful day at Columbine High School would come true: *"I'm going to have an impact on the world."*

Less than 30 minutes later, as Rachel sat on the grass on the backside of the school, eating lunch with her friend, Richard Castaldo, she would die from a gunshot blast as Eric Harris, one of her classmates, put a gun to her head and pulled the trigger.

But before he pulled the trigger, he asked her a question that you will learn more about later in this book.

Chapter 2
THE DIARIES
(Some writings are photoshopped for clarity or length. Content hasn't been changed)

The story about Anne Frank and her diary would inspire millions of young people in the decades following her death in a Nazi prison camp. Rachel told me that she was motivated to keep diaries because of Anne Frank. Our family has all 6 of Rachel's diaries, and we have read them over and over, many times.

Her first diary was a Christmas present from her mom, Beth Nimmo.

December 25, 97

Dear God,
Thank you!!! Thank you for my mom, my mom who gave me this journal so that I may write you. Thank you for my family, my friends, and my youth. my words will be said to you thru my writings I write to you now thanking you. Today we recognize the birth of your Son, Jesus. I thank you for Him. He was born to us, so that He may die for us. Thank you. I love you Father. I love you because of your grace, your righteosness, your forgiveness, your love.
Amen

Over the next 18 months she would fill up 6 diaries - - and many of her words would be addressed to God. One of these diaries was shared with her cousin, Jeff Scott, and another one was shared with her friend, Mark Bodiford.

Mark was a somewhat homeless young man who, at the time, viewed himself as an outcast from society. He was covered with tattoos and was a part of a heavy metal band. He credited Rachel for saving his life through her kindness and friendship.

On the cover of Rachel's final diary, you can learn a lot about her views of life and her personality.

Rachel wrote quite a bit about dreams and purpose. She seemed to
be tuned in to destiny as she wrote the following in her diary:

> Dreaming...
>
> I close my eyes
> I open my mind
> I think of things
> Yet to come
> Until that day
> Will come to be
> I close my eyes
> And dream a dream.

You may, or may not, believe that God allows people to have a sense
of purpose in their lives, but it seems evident to me that my daughter
had a strong prophetic sense of her purpose on this planet. She wasn't
sure how it was going to unfold - - but she was sure that it would!

In the above diary entry, she wrote that until the day of unfolding
came, she would simply close her eyes and dream a dream.

2 Timothy 1:9 says that God called us with his own purpose in mind
before the ages even began! Some people seemed to be tapped into
their purpose more than others.

Rachel had an urgent sense of purpose, and a belief that someday the
world would see what God had placed in her. She understood that
her personal faith played a role in the fulfilment of what God
intended for her life. She wrote, in two different places, that she could
reach that purpose by believing and accepting it.

In the 2 entries below she expressed her faith in reaching the dreams that God had put in her.

Don't put limits on what I can do
I have faith, why can't you

Don't keep me from my dreams
I can reach them if I believe

So, when she declared, on the cover of that final diary, that she was writing for the sake of her soul - - she meant it! Many of her friends testified about her passion for God and her love for others at her funeral. That passion has lived on decades after her death and is still empowering people to enter the spiral of her rose, ascending to a higher place.

But her next writing reveals, not only her dream and purpose, but also hinted at the possibility of an early death.

Things untold
Things unseen
One day all these things
Will come to me.

Life of meaning
Life of hope
Life of significance
Is mine to cope.

I have a purpose
I have a dream
I have a future
So it seems

26

Paul wrote in 2 Corinthians 4:18, *"So we fix our eyes not on what is seen, but on what is unseen, since what is seen is temporary, but what is unseen is eternal."*

Rachel was hearing things untold and seeing things unseen, knowing that the day would come when all those things would be manifested in this present world. She wrote, *"One day all this things will come to me."*

She ends this entry with the words, *"I have a future"* - - but then adds, almost tentatively - - *"so it seems."* Adding those last 3 words puts a question mark around her future.

As you will read about later, she had a strong premonition that her life would be short, but meaningful. Maybe that's why she wrote, *"I write for the sake of my soul"* on the front of her last diary. Above that powerful statement she wrote:

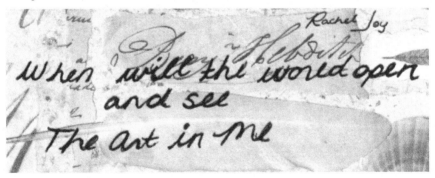

There was a yearning in Rachel for her inner purpose, her "art", to be seen by the world. In her 17 years of life, she was not famous or well-known.

She was the middle child of a lower middle-class family, working part time at a Subway sandwich shop, and driving a used Honda Legend to school. She had no way of knowing that, she too, would become a legend one day.

Just as Anne Frank died, not knowing that the world would read her diary and hear her story, Rachel could not possibly have known about the impact that her life would have on millions and millions of people after her death. And yet, there seemed to be an intuitive, prophetic sense that her life would make a difference in this world.

Jesus endured the suffering and shame of the cross because of the glory that would be revealed afterward and for the joy that it would produce. He knew that he would be crowned with glory and honor. But he also knew that the cross would come before the crown.

"For the joy set before him, he endured the cross, scorning its shame, and sat down at the right hand of the throne of God." Heb. 12:2 NIV

I am by no means comparing Rachel to Jesus or trying to make her experience appear to be the same as his, but the principle is the same. Rachel expressed her willingness to do, as she wrote, *"whatever it takes"* to reach the unreached.

One year and one month before she was shot and killed at Columbine, she wrote the following in her diary:

3/1/98

Dear God,
I want to feel you in my heart, mind, soul, and life. I want heads to turn in the halls when I walk by. I want them to stare at me, watching and wanting the light you have put in me. I want You to overflow my cup with your Spirit. I want so much from you. I want you to use me to reach the unreached. I have such a desire and passion to serve, but I want to do that now

28

You can feel the urgency in her writing when she says, *"I have such a desire and passion to serve, but I want to do that now."* She did not want to wait until she was older, or more mature. The sense of destiny in her can also be felt in the following diary entry:

People are crying,
Losing their minds.
People are dying,
Taking their lives.
Will anyone save them?
Will anyone help?
Will somebody listen,
Or am I all by myself?

She asked the question on the cover of her diary, *"When will the world open and see the art in me?"* She knew that day was coming, but she just didn't know when, so she asked the following question inside of her diary:

When can I unlock the door and see
The path that leads to my destiny

She answered that question in the following entry:

One day the world will see
What I know burns inside of me

29

But, like every human being that has ever lived, Rachel was tested at times. She had her times of doubt, confusion, and failure. Several entries in her diary expressed times of depression and self-doubt. In this entry she writes about shifting emotions and confusion:

As emotions shift,
Decisions drift.
As confusion clouds
Unsureness bounds
All things are hazed, distorted, & out of focus
My heart is numb, twisted, and broken
How can I give
How can I receive
Nothing can be asked
Or given to me

It is so important for you to see that Rachel was someone who had her own doubts and fears. Here, she writes about her insecurities:

Why can't I be used by you? Why do I feel self-righteouse at times? Why do I feel afraid?

In this entry Rachel writes to God about how people look at her and think she has it together. But as you can see, she was experiencing turmoil on the inside, as she pleads with God to take her to a whole new level:

I stand back, God, and I watch those around me and ask myself, What is it that they're feeling? What is it that they're thinking? Are they seeing you? Can they hear you? If so, why can't I? What am I doing so wrong that I can't reach that level? Everyone looks at me and thinks wow, what a together kinda girl. She's doing good But you know God that I'm not. Why won't you fix that? I don't understand. This feeling is killing me, God. Why don't you do something? I know that you have already done so much, but why stop there? I want to reach a new level with you God. Take me there. Please, God, take me there. I want that so much. I want to serve you. I want to be used by you to help others. But I feel like I can't do that until you change this feeling I have. Come to me God, and make use of me.

Your servant,
Rachel Joy

31

A short time before she died, Rachel had started writing a book that she never got to finish. One chapter was titled, *"What Do I Do About God?"* In it, she talked about her ups and downs, and she left a challenge for us all to embrace:

"I had my UPS and downs and I fell a few times, but I did not give up. Don't give up, because God's reward is worth it all. ... I challenge you to listen, and see what God will do. Take a risk, chance it, trust in God. ... You will see what God can do with a willing heart."

—Rachel Scott

From a chapter titled, "What do I do about God?" for a book Rachel was in the process of writing

In Hebrews chapter 11 there is a list of what are called, "the heroes of faith." It honors Gideon, who was a coward. It honors Rahab, who was a harlot. It honors Sampson, who was a womanizer. It honors David, who was a murderer and an adulterer.

These men and women were not listed as "heroes of faith" because of their failures - - but in spite of their failures - - they did not give up. Their faith took them past the valleys of depression, despair, adultery, prostitution, and murder. They recognized their weaknesses and continued to believe that God could use them, despite their human flaws and failures.

Although Rachel has been gone for many years, I hope that her words are alive for you today. In the middle of your "ups and downs" I hope that you will not give up. Rachel challenged all of us to take a risk, trust in God, and see what he can do with a willing heart!

Chapter 3
THE FORK IN THE ROAD

The third thing that Rachel wrote on the cover of her final diary was:

Many decades ago, Robert Frost wrote a poem called, *"The Road Not Taken"*, that has inspired many people. I don't know if Rachel was aware of that poem or not, but the first and last paragraphs of his poem set the stage for her statement. Here are Robert Frost's first and last stanzas.

THE ROAD NOT TAKEN

Two roads diverged in a yellow wood,
And sorry I could not travel both
And be one traveler, long I stood
And looked down one as far as I could
To where it bent in the undergrowth

I shall be telling this with a sigh
Somewhere ages and ages hence:
Two roads converged in a wood, and I –
I took the one less traveled by
And that has made all the difference

Rachel wrote about standing at the fork in the road and taking *neither* path! Instead, she let her mind create stories yet untold. She chose a third path in her mind - - not just a path less traveled, but a path that no one had traveled before! It was not a matter of one or the other - - she made a third choice, where no one had ever gone before.

She amplified her decision from a passage in her diary:

> Standing at a crossroad,
> Two paths to take,
>   Expected to choose
> The path to my fate.
>
>   If it's all the same
>   to you, world...
> Neither is my choice.
>
> Why not stand here
>   at the fork in the road,
> And let my mind
>   Create the stories untold.

Too often, in politics, religion, and education, we are given only two choices. We must choose between pro-life or pro-choice. We are either for gun control or we are against it. Theologically, we are either Calvinistic or Armenian. We either believe in freewill or predestination. We are for public education or against it.

But what if there is a third choice?

Like Rachel, we often stand at the fork in the road trying to decide which direction to take. Do we go to the right or to the left? For most of us, there seems to be no third choice. It's either/or, - - or, neither/nor.

Few take the road less traveled. Even fewer take neither of the two roads. Rachel's poetry about standing at the fork in the road inspired me to write the following poem several years after her death.

THE ROAD UNTRAVELED

I traveled down the broadest road where masses choose to go
I found it safe, but boring - - methodical and slow
Its well-worn tracks and markers, all guiding me ahead
Where lifeless travelers move along like crowds of walking dead

But then I found another path, less traveled than the rest
Not safe – but more exciting – a challenging new quest
And then one day I realized that there was even more
A place beyond "less traveled" where no one had gone before

Excitement raced inside my veins and purpose filled my heart
There were no footprints up ahead where I would have to start
I knew without a single doubt, this path was just for me
With faith – and fear, I took a step, toward my destiny

I saw and heard things yet untold – and moved in realms unknown
Down paths of risk and treasure where no one had ever gone
The road less traveled, though it's grand, my friend cannot compare
To one intended just for you, when purpose calls you there

No eye has seen, no ear has heard the treasures that await
Regardless of decisions past, it never is too late
Be not afraid to take that step that leads to destiny
For only the untraveled road will set you spirit free!

"Eye has not seen, nor ear heard, nor have entered into the heart of man the things God has prepared for those who love him."

1 Corinthians 2:9 NIV

The untraveled road will lead us to fulfillment, peace, joy, and contentment. The broad way used by the masses leads to destruction. The narrow, untraveled way leads to life! Unfortunately, "few there be that find it."

The Bible verse that talks about a strait gate and narrow way is usually misunderstood. Most think it leads to heaven, but that's not what it says. It says the narrow way leads to life - - here and now!

"For my thoughts are not your thoughts, neither are your ways, my ways." Isaiah 55:8-9 NIV

Albert Einstein once said, *"We cannot solve our problems with the same level of thinking that created them."* That is why we must experience a "renewing of our mind." There must be a transformation in our thinking.

Rachel dared to think outside the box. She dared to ask questions that not many people ask. She refused to be a puppet, manipulated by the opinion of her peers.

That takes us to the 4th statement on the cover of her diary:

"If you don't want to be the puppet on strings - - Don't play the dummy."

She wrote this upside down in the left bottom corner of her diary cover.

36

Rachel refused to be "put in a box" socially. She had a reputation at her school for reaching out to people that were often neglected or disabled. She also refused to follow the current trends in what she wore.

She was an individualist when it came to her dresses, her pants, her shirts, her shoes, and whatever she happened to put on top of her head on any given day!

She loved her hats, and she wore a variety of different hats to school. Her younger brother, Mike, also was a "hat wearer." Even today, decades later, Mike can be seen in baseball caps or British driving caps. At Christmas, both Mike and Rachel were always thrilled to get new caps or hats.

QR Code: Mike about Rachel's hats

The first time I appeared on the Oprah Show to honor Rachel's memory, Oprah put up this picture of Rachel, and talked about her fondness for wearing hats.

Her friends represented a wide variety of different types of people. There was Mark Bodiford, the tattooed, homeless guy; Adam, the special needs student who was often bullied; Val, the tough girl who was taking drugs, Sergio, who was struggling with his sexual identity, and Brooks Brown, who had been a close friend of the shooters, Eric and Dylan. Listen to what Brooks had to say about Rachel:

QR Code: Brooks Brown about Rachel

She loved them all equally and treated them with respect. She was not the dummy puppet who was controlled by the strings of fads and opinions.

The 5th and final writing on the cover of her diary are the words, *"If you will not take credit in my failures, you will not be given credit in my success."*

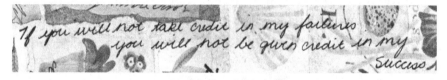

Rachel was extremely loyal to her friends. She accepted them unconditionally - - which is what "agape" love is all about. There are 3 Greek words in the Bible for love: Eros, phileo, and agape.

From the word "eros" we get the word, "erotic." This is a selfish form of "love" that uses people without giving anything in return. People who operate in eros, do not understand the meaning of true friendship. They only use people to get what they want from them.

From the word "phileo," we get words like philanthropist or Philadelphia. Phileo love is what most friendships and marriages are based on. It is a give and take relationship based on mutual trust. The city of Philadelphia means, "brotherly love" and got its origin from the word "phileo."

However, the deepest realm of love is "agape." It is completely unconditional, expecting nothing in return. It gives with no expectation of getting something back. The person practicing agape is a "giver", not a "taker." This is demonstrated in John 3:16: "For God so loved that world that he gave - - -."

Rachel was not happy with people who were not loyal to their friends. She didn't approve of hypocritical behavior. She wrote in her "Codes of Life" (*we will look at that later*) that *"trust and honesty is an investment you put in people."*

Here's a small portion of her "Codes of Life" where she talks about honesty and trust:

> I have been told repeatedly that I trust people too easily, but I find that when I put my faith and trust in people when others would not dare to, they almost never betray me would hope that people would put that same faith in me. Trust and honesty is an investment you put in people; if you build enough trust in them and show yourself to be honest, they will do the same in you. I value honesty so much, and it is an expectation I have of myself. I will put honesty before the risk of humiliation, before selfishness, and before anything less worthy of the Gospel truth. Even in being honest and trust worthy, I do not come off cold and heartless. Compassion and honesty go hand in hand, if enough of each is put into every situation. I admire those who trust and are trust worthy.

So, when she wrote, *"If you will not take credit in my failures, you will not be given credit in my success,"* she practiced that in her relationship with others. She was there for them in their failures as well as their success.

An example of that was her interaction with a young man named Adam. He was a special ed student who was born with a disease that caused him to look different, act different, and talk different from other students. Adam did not have any friends at Columbine and would often sit by himself in the cafeteria - - ignored by others.

He was often picked on and made fun of by other students. The first time Rachel met him was in a hallway at school. Two boys had knocked his books out of his hands and were laughing at him as they shoved him up against some lockers.

Rachel saw what was happening and she was furious! She ran up and got between those two boys and Adam, doubled up her fists - - and said, *"if you don't leave him alone, you're going to have to fight me!"*

Now, I'm sure that they were scared out of their minds - - looking at this little girl who was half their size, threatening them. They were probably thinking, *"If we beat her up, we're going to look bad! But if she beats us up, we're really going to look bad!"* So, they backed off and Rachel became a friend to Adam.

(To hear Adam talk about how Rachel impacted his life use the **QR** code below)

After Rachel was killed, Adam became a friend to our entire family. He told us that Rachel's kindness saved his life from suicide. He had planned to take his life, because he felt like no one cared about him, until Rachel came along.

We invited Adam to join our team in 2000 when we launched our school program. Sandy and I took a small group of Columbine students along with my remaining children, and we went to El Paso, Texas where we did presentations in 40 schools in one week!

Adam was not a speaker, but he went to the schools with our presenters and told the students how Rachel had saved his life.

Two of my close friends, Paul Jackson, and Bill Sanders, helped me train our team. After just one day of training, we sent them into all the middle and high schools in the El Paso area, and at the end of the week I gave a presentation in the civic center for all the parents and educators.

Paul Jackson (left)
and
Bill Sanders (right)
working on the
team's scripts

Over the years, Paul and Bill would remain an integral part of our school program, *Rachel's Challenge.*

Paul would be our team manager and travel with Sandy and I to many of those early events in churches, colleges, schools, and outdoor stadiums. Paul was the manager for the famous Oak Ridge Boys and later managed the Christian group, Petra. Then he became an assistant to Josh McDowell before joining our organization.

Bill, who was trained by Zig Ziglar as a speaker, became a presenter for *Rachel's Challenge.*

41

Below is a picture of our El Paso presenters. Adam is the one wearing a cowboy hat. Nicole, at the bottom right, still had a bullet in her body from the shootings at Columbine. My oldest son, Craig, is at the top. My daughters, Bethanee and Dana are in the second row from top. My youngest son, Mike, is in the third row on the right wearing a cap. *(Remember what I said about Rachel and Mike loving hats?)*

Josh Weidman is now a pastor. He is on the bottom left. Next to him is Sarah, one of Rachel's closest friends. In the center is Scott Dodge, who became the first full time speaker for *Rachel's Challenge.*

And finally, the Cohen brothers, Stephen, and Jonathan. One is next to Josh, and the other is just above him. They wrote and sang a song called, "Columbine, Friend of Mine" that was played across the nation after the tragedy. You can hear it on YouTube.

Because Rachel stood at the fork in the road and let her mind create the stories yet untold, she, like Abel in Hebrews 11:4, "being dead -- yet speaks!" She didn't live to see all the untold stories of lives saved and school shootings prevented.

42

Chapter 4
RACHEL'S CODES OF LIFE

A few days before Rachel died, her English teacher, Mrs. Caruthers (yes, the same one), gave an assignment to the class. The assignment was to write a short essay on any subject that the students wanted to write about. Rachel titled her essay: My Ethics, My Codes of Life.

My Ethics, My Codes of Life
Rachel Scott

Ethics vary with environment, circumstances, and culture. In my own life, ethics play a major role. Whether it was because of the way I was raised, the experiences I've had, or just my outlook on the world and the way things should be. My biggest aspects of ethics include being honest, compassionate, and looking for the best and beauty in everyone.

I have been told repeatedly that I trust people too easily, but I find that when I put my faith and trust in people when others would not dare to, they almost never betray me. I would hope that people would put that same faith in me. Trust and honesty is an investment you put in people; if you build enough trust in them and show yourself to be honest, they will do the same in you. I value honesty so much, and it is an expectation I have of myself. I will put honesty before the risk of humiliation, before selfishness, and before anything less worthy of the Gospel truth. Even in being honest and trust worth, I do not come off cold and heartless. Compassion and honesty go hand in hand, if enough of each is put into every situation. I admire those who trust and are trust worthy.

Compassion is the greatest form of love humans have to offer. According to Webster's Dictionary compassion means a feeling of sympathy for another's misfortune. My definition of compassion is forgiving, loving, helping, leading, and showing mercy for others. I have this theory that if one person can go out of their way to show compassion, then it will start a chain reaction of the same. People will never know how far a little kindness can go.

43

It wasn't until recently that I learned that the first and the second and the third impressions can be deceitful of what kind of person someone is. For example, imagine you had just met someone, and you speak with them three times on brief everyday conversations. They come off as a harsh, cruel, stubborn, and ignorant person. You reach your judgment based on just these three encounters. Let me ask you something...did you ever ask them what their goal in life is, what kind of past they came from, did they experience love, did they experience hurt, did you look into their soul and not just at their appearance? Until you know them and not just their "type," you have no right to shun them. You have not looked for their beauty, their good. You have not seen the light in their eyes. Look hard enough and you will always find a light, and you can even help it grow, if you don't walk away from those three impressions first.

I am sure that my codes of life may be very different from yours, but how do you know that trust, compassion, and beauty will not make this world a better place to be in and this life a better one to live? My codes may seem like a fantasy that can never be reached, but test them for yourself, and see the kind of effect they have in the lives of people around you. You just may start a chain reaction.

Today, many young people have read Rachel's Codes of Life and have adopted them as their own. This essay became the foundation of our organization, *Rachel' Challenge*, which has impacted the lives of millions of lives around the world.

There are so many powerful statements in this essay, but I want to just highlight a few of them. She starts out by writing that her biggest aspects of her own ethics are honesty, compassion, and looking for the best in others.

She goes on to describe what it means to look for the best in others. She wrote that the first three encounters we have with someone may be deceitful. She encouraged us not to judge people by those first three encounters. She admitted that they may *appear* to be harsh, cruel, stubborn, or ignorant - - but she challenged us not to judge them by those first three impressions!

She goes on to write, *"did you look into their soul, and not just at their appearance!"*

Rachel learned this from a lesson that I had received from a mentor in my life. His name was Norman Grubb. Norman was a World War I veteran of the British army and had received medals for his valor and his wounds in that terrible war.

After the horror of that war that claimed over 37 million lives, Norman became a man of peace. He wrote many bestsellers in the 1940's and 1950's. He spent twenty years of his life in the African Congo as a missionary, working with his father-in-law, the famous C.T. Studd.

Norman became a mentor in my life when I was 22 years old.

He taught me something that I passed on to my children - - and you can see it reflected in Rachel's Codes of Life. He said, "Darrell, if you will learn to be a "SEE-THROUGHER" instead of a "LOOK-ATTER," life will have purpose and meaning."

He went on to say, "*Don't look at your circumstances - - learn to see through them, and on the worst days of your life you will find purpose. Don't look at people - - learn to see through their appearance and look at their heart. When you are a see-througher life becomes more fulfilling and meaningful.*"

After Rachel died, Norman's life lesson and Rachel's Codes of Life helped get our family through the horror of that tragedy. We chose to be see-throughers and not look-atters.

Norman Grubb  **Rachel**

Today our presenters for Rachel's Challenge tell the story of Norman Grubb and the lesson he taught our family

Watch this video about being a "See-Througher"

As Rachel practiced this principle at her school, she began to see through the appearances of others. She began to recognize their needs and went out of her way to help meet them.

In her Codes of Life she wrote, "*I have this theory, that if one person can go out of their way to show compassion - - it will start a chain reaction of the same. People will never know how far a little kindness can go.*"

It doesn't take a crowd, or a few, or even a couple of people to start a chain reaction of kindness. It only takes one!

She went on to write: *"My codes may seem like a fantasy that can never be reached, but test them for yourself, and see the kind of effect they have in the people around you. You may just start a chain reaction!"*

This part of her Codes of Life sparked a whole new program that we call, "Chain Reaction." To see more about that check out the **QR** code below:

Celebrities would be encouraged to accept Rachel's challenge to start a chain reaction of kindness, including Clark Hunt, the owner of the Kansas City Chiefs, Glenn Close, Reba McEntire, Chuck Norris, Elton John, Lee Greenwood, and many more.

Listen to Clark Hunt, owner of the Kansas City Chiefs talk about *Rachel's Challenge:*

Rachel's desire to start a chain reaction of kindness has become a reality. Her Codes of Life are practiced by many people. *Rachel's Challenge* not only has a full day program called, "Chain Reaction", but schools around the world celebrate acts of kindness with paper chains - - each link of the chain representing an act of kindness that has been performed by a student, teacher, or parent.

These celebrations of kindness take place in football stadiums, soccer fields, sports arenas, auditoriums, and outdoors. They usually take place near the end of the school year to be celebrated with links the acts of kindness that have been recorded throughout the school year. Below is an example of one of those celebrations.

In Rockwell, Texas, in 2010, Dr. Gene Burton, who was the Superintendent of Schools, got his entire city involved. They created a chain of kindness that was 27 miles long, representing the acts of kindness in all the Rockwell schools that year!

Here is Sandy and I lying in just a few of the chain links at that event:

Before the celebration in Rockwall, all the students had gone to several large buildings and packaged meals for people in Haiti who were starving to death. A massive earthquake had killed over 300,000 people and left millions without food and water.

The students broke a world record by packaging over 1 million meals in 7 hours! Watch the amazing video below to see what happened:

On November 11, 2011, the city of Atlanta, Georgia hosted a celebration of kindness in the Georgia Dome. The date was chosen so that it would be called 11-11-11, hosted by NBC, channel 11.

The Atlanta NBC television station helped us reach out to all the schools in Atlanta and co-ordinate the event. The Georgia Dome was packed with students, parents, and educators celebrating *Rachel's Challenge* and acts of kindness in their schools all year long.

Large cranes lifted the paper chain links to the ceiling and the entire event was a joyous celebration!

Here is a close-up picture of the chains of kindness that was at the top of the previous picture in the Georgia Dome:

To see a part of that celebration go to the **QR Code** below:

As a result of that event in Atlanta, *Rachel's Challenge* would go on to receive a television Emmy Award from that NBC affiliate.

This is only one of three Emmys that were awarded because of Rachel's story.

The other two were in Seattle, Washington and Phoenix, AZ.

Chapter 5
THE BACK OF RACHEL'S FINAL DIARY

Now, let's take a look at what Rachel wrote on the back of her final diary:

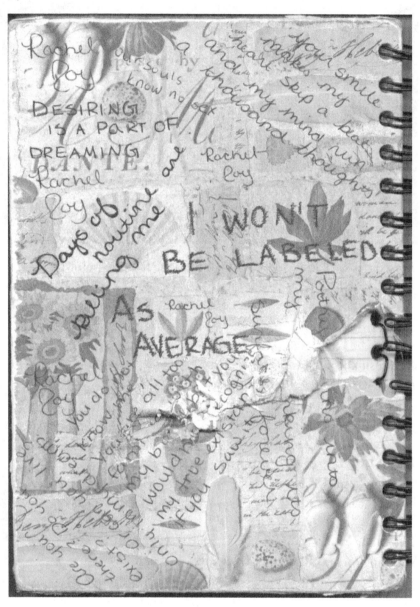

In the upper left corner she wrote her name, followed by two statements. The first is slanted to the right and says: *"Our souls know no sex."*

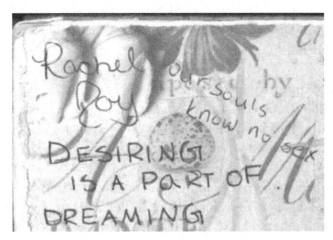

This may seem to be a very strange statement for Rachel to write on the back cover of her diary, but it reveals that she had reflected deeply on the true essence of a person and the need to be a see-througher and not a look-atter.

Perhaps she wrote this after reading a passage in the Bible from Galatians 3:28, *"Ther is neither Jew nor Gentile, neither slave nor free, nor is there male and female, for you are all one in Christ Jesus."* She refused to reject people because of their gender, their color, their ethnic origin, or their sexual orientation. Rachel knew the difference between approval and acceptance.

Her opinion about whether someone was right or wrong on an issue was not a hindrance in her acceptance of others. When Jesus said, *"Love your neighbor as yourself"* he did not say to find out what they believed or practiced before loving them.

This is an issue that I believe organized religion is going to have to honestly face and deal with. Rachel practiced agape love that allowed her to embrace people of all appearances and opinions.

Rachel knew that connection and relationships with others was far more important than rejection or compromise.

On February 11, 2018, 19-year-old Nikolas Cruz shot and killed 17 people at Marjory Stoneman Douglas High School in Parkland, Florida. He left 17 others wounded.

President Trump, who I had met with previously, asked for Sandy and I to attend a meeting at the White House along with victims' families from Parkland. The event was on every major network and news channel, and was seen around the world.

The President asked me to address the people in attendance and the worldwide audience. I was thinking of Rachel and her ability to connect with others, and so what I said, in essence, was the following:

"When we meet others that we disagree with we have 3 choices. We can hate and retaliate, we can debate and demonstrate, or we can relate and communicate. If we can communicate with each other in a civilized manner, we may create an atmosphere in which we can relate, and perhaps even become friends. If we focus too much on diversity, we create division. If we focus too much on unity, we create compromise. When we learn to relate, we can celebrate diversity and work toward unity, avoiding division and compromise."

Darrell Scott with President Trump in the White House

54

After the meeting was over, Vice-President Pence came over and asked me if he could use my statements at a meeting he would be speaking at the next day, and I cheerfully agreed. Below is a picture of Vice-President Pence holding a picture of Rachel, with Sandy and me.

Rachel's words from her Codes of Life have become a reality: *"People will never know how far a little kindness can go."*

Her second statement on the back of her diary was, *"Desiring is a part of dreaming."* I have heard many people refer to Rachel as *"an old soul"*, and I believe she was. Her wisdom was much deeper than her age or experiences could have possibly produced.

She recognized that true purpose comes from dreaming, and that dreaming is fueled by valid desire. We saw earlier that she wrote, *"I have such a desire and passion to serve, but I want to do that now."*

Psalm 37:4 says, *"Delight yourself in the Lord, and he will give you the desires of your heart."* Rachel 's heart desire was to reach the unreached and her short life did not prevent that from happening. She was proof that, *"Desiring is a part of dreaming."*

On the upper right corner of her diary she wrote:

In 1883, Ella Wheeler Wilcox wrote in her poem, "Solitude," the words: *"Laugh and the world laughs with you - - weep, and you weep alone."* Rachel had a contagious smile that brought joy to everyone she met.

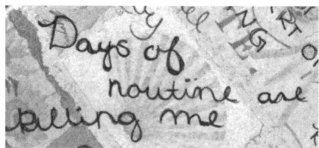

This is an absolute reflection of Rachel's personality. She hated the status quo, and she hated routine days.

In the center of the back of her diary, she wrote:

Cal Ripken Jr. is one of the most famous baseball players in history. He is a Hall of Fame member and holds the sports record that all experts agree will never be broken. Cal played in 2,632 consecutive games over 17 years, breaking Lou Gehrig's record by over 500!

Cal loved this statement by Rachel, *"I Won't Be Labeled As Average"* and our organizations began to work together in reaching many more young people.

Cal Ripken and his team joined together with *Rachel's Challenge* and created a program called, "The Uncommon Athlete" based on Rachel's statement on the back of her diary.

Darrell   Sandy   Cal Ripken, Jr.

The Cal Ripken, Sr. Foundation was dedicated by Cal and his brother Bill to the memory of their father, Cal Ripken, Sr., who was a coach for the Baltimore Orioles while both of his sons played on the team!

Listen to this amazing video where Bill Ripken talks about the partnership between *Rachel's Challenge* and the *Cal Ripken, Sr. Foundation.* The theme is "The Uncommon Athlete."

Rachel's message on the back of her diary would go on to inspire thousands of young athletes who participated in "The Uncommon Athlete" program.

A dear friend, Joe Coles, helped us develop the content for that program and presented it to many students.

Beside the words, *"I won't be labeled as average,"* you can see a hole in her diary where a bullet entered as though it's an exclamation mark to that statement.

The Columbine tragedy was a clash between good and evil that day. It would appear to many that evil won, but hindsight causes others to see a different picture. Although the loss of 13 innocent lives cannot be underestimated, each year, *Rachel's Challenge* receives communication from around 150 students who were planning to commit suicide and changed their mind after attending an assembly or training session.

Today, millions of young people have taken up the mantra, *"I won't be labeled as average."*

The next writing on the back of her diary was damaged by a bullet hole. It obliterated a few of the letters in the line that she wrote on the back of her diary.

The readable part says, *"Poetry ***ns into my ***, *nking its surfaces forever."* My own interpretation of this is, *"Poetry burns into my heart, inking its surfaces forever."* What a poetic way of defining poetry!

Rachel's writings were very poetic. She, perhaps, inherited that poetic gift from me. I don't mean that egotistically, but the fact is, I have written over a thousand poems, of which most have been published. I won a national contest at age 11 with the first poem I wrote.

In Rachel's memory, I wrote a book called, "Thirsty Fish", available on Amazon, that features 150 of my poems. Many of them were inspired by Rachel and her writings. Here's one example:

IN THE QUIET
by: Darrell Scott

In the quiet I find peace
Where the outside noises cease

When my mind has settled down
And my thoughts no longer race
In the chambers of my spirit
I have found a secret place

There the unseen things embrace us
The invisible that's real
And we there enjoy the treasures
That activity would steal

Hear the whisper of the poets
As they beckon us to know
Of that inner sanctuary
Where we seldom ever go

In the quiet of my being
Creativity is born
And it rises to the surface
To a world that's hurt and torn

Deep within me love replaces
All the anger and the fear
In the stillness is a knowing
Who I am - - - and why I'm here!

You can see segments of her writing scattered all the way through this poem. For example, my line in the poem: *"There the unseen things embrace us"* was inspired by this writing from Rachel's diaries:

> Things untold
> Things unseen
> One day all these things
> Will come to me.

In my poem I wrote, *"Of that inner sanctuary where we seldom ever go."* This was a take-off from what she wrote in her diary, just one month before she was killed:

> March 25, 99
> God, you know my goals,
> my dreams. But I cannot reach them
> without you. I need your help.
> Let me find you without the need of
> a church. Create in me the church,
> so that where ever I go, I will
> find sanctuary.
>
> Rachel Joy

Rachel realized that she could find sanctuary without the need of a church building. She wasn't criticizing church buildings, because attended one.

She was talking about God creating within her a sanctuary where she could find fellowship with him outside of Sunday mornings and Wednesday nights.

She knew what Jesus said to the Pharisees was true. *"The kingdom of God does not come with observation. Nor will they say, 'See here', or 'See there'; for indeed, the kingdom of God is within you."*

The next writing on the back of her diary expressed her sadness that others chose to be look-atters instead of see-throughers. This writing was also damaged by the bullet that entered her diary. She wrote, *"You do not know me. You are all too familiar with my body, but you would not recognize my true existence if you saw it."*

Rachel often felt alone in her quest to be a see-througher, and to reach out and help the unreached. Remember when she wrote, *"Will anyone save them, will anyone help? Will anyone listen, or am I all by myself?"*

This was also an extension of what she wrote on the front of this diary: *"When will the world open and see the art in me."* Many times we fail to appreciate and recognize people until after we lose them.

Henry David Thoreau wrote, *"It's not what you look at, but what you see."* Jesus said, *"You have eyes to see but cannot see; ears to hear but you cannot hear."* And, Hellen Keller, who was blind, deaf and speech impaired wrote: *"The only thing worse than being blind, is having sight but no vision."*

The last thing she wrote on the back of her diary can be found in the lower left side. Since it was written upside down, I photoshopped it and turned it right side up to make it easier to read.

Every believer has walked through the valley of questioning and doubt at one time or another. Here, Rachel was questioning whether God really existed of if he was just living in her dreams.

You can see here, desperation, in one of her writings below:

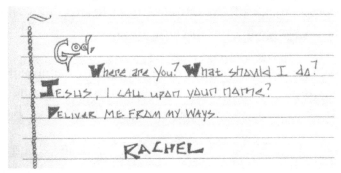

It is important that people do not put Rachel on such a pedestal that she appears perfect. She would be the first to admit that she was flawed and that her faith was tested at times. I Peter 4:12 says, *"Beloved, do not think it strange concerning the fiery trial which is to try you, as though some strange thing happened to you."*

Chapter 6
THE FINAL ROSE

Now let's go back to the fourth and final rose that Rachel drew on the last day of her life. After completing the drawing, she placed her diary in her backpack and headed out for lunch.

We did not have access to her final two diaries until seven weeks after the tragedy at Columbine. The sheriff's department had kept her backpack as evidence because there were several bullet holes in it.

We suspected that her final diaries were in that backpack, but we didn't know for sure.

Six weeks following Rachel's death I got the strangest phone call I had ever received in my life. A man I had never met or heard of, by the name of Frank Amedia called me with a very odd message. Frank lived in Youngstown, Ohio where he was a successful businessman.

He told me that he had been having the same dream every night for the last week and it was about my daughter's eyes. He said that in the dream he saw a trickle of tears dripping from Rachel's eyes and they were watering something that was growing out of the ground.

Frank asked me if that meant anything to me or my family, and I told him *"No, it didn't."* He then asked if I would write his phone number down and call me if it meant anything to anyone who knew Rachel.

I was very skeptical about Frank's story, but I went ahead and wrote his phone number, thinking that I would never be talking to him again. Listen to Frank tell what happened:

Another week went by, and I received a phone call from the sheriff's department. They told me that they had Rachel's backpack, and I was free to pick it up.

I rushed over to get it with my heart pounding and emotions surging through me. As I carried it out to my truck, I noticed several bullet holes as well as blood stains. My heart was so saddened as I reflected on those last few moments of her life.

Rachel's Backpack

When a parent loses a child, they often cling to their articles of clothing, their toys, or anything associated with their child. For us, Rachel's backpack and diaries provided that connection.

When I got to my truck, I opened her backpack and found her schoolbooks, some rubber bands, combs, and other random items that a teenage girl would have. But what I was hoping to find was up against the side of her backpack - - her final two diaries!

I quickly turned to the last page of her final diary, hoping to read the last words she recorded before she died.

But I was in for a shock! When I turned to the last page, instead of another diary entry, I was looking at a picture she had drawn.

And you guessed it - - - it was the drawing of her final rose! I was doubly shocked, because this was exactly what Frank had described to me in a dream!

Notice that her eyes were producing a trickle of tears that are falling around a rose that was growing out of a Columbine flower. In this picture you can't see the Columbine, but it is seen in her second rose drawing.

When I got home, I went to my desk and dug out Frank's phone number and called him. I asked if he had a fax machine and he said, "Yes." I faxed over the picture, and he called me back and he was sobbing. He said that Rachel's drawing was exactly what he had seen in that repetitive dream he had experienced.

I counted 13 clear tears falling from her eyes before they turned dark when they touched the rose. 13 people were murdered at Columbine within a couple of hours after she drew this picture.

I sat in my truck weeping as I looked at this picture. I had an intuitive feeling that there was more to this than just the picture. Over the next 25 years that feeling would prove to be true!

For years I thought the dark drops were blood drops, as I mentioned in the first chapter. But I was speaking at a large educational conference a few years ago and a young teacher walked up to me and said, *"Mr. Scott, I don't think those are blood drops - - I think they are seeds. I think her tears are turning into seeds."*

I asked, *"What makes you think that?"* She replied, *"Because when Frank called and told you his dream, he saw her tears watering something that was growing out of the ground. Blood drops don't make things grow out of the ground, but seeds do! I think her tears were turning into seeds."*

That was an "aha" moment for me and I agreed with her. The seeds from Rachel's tears have been planted in the hearts of millions of people and will bear fruit for many years to come. But that was not the end of the tears story.

About 6 months after the tragedy, I began to get requests to speak at large gatherings all over the nation and around the world.

Most of these were from Christian groups that were deeply moved by Rachel's faith and her last words (which we will look at later).

One of those events was in Jackson, Tennessee. The owners of the Old Country Store were the hosts of the event. The Old Country Store was the model for all the Cracker Barrel restaurants.

Churches from miles around brought their folding chairs to an open field right outside the store. Around 8,000 people showed up to hear Rachel's story.

Huge speakers and amplifiers were placed in strategic locations so that everyone could hear. There was no screen or projector, so I simply told her story without any illustrations or video.

Near the end of my presentation, I told the story of Frank and the drawing of Rachel's tears for the first time in a public venue.

When I began describing Rachel's drawing, a young girl about 17 years old, who was sitting on the left side started crying. A lot of people cried when they heard Rachel's story, but this young girl was just sobbing loudly.

When I finished speaking, she was the first one to run up to talk with me, and she said, *"Mr. Scott, I didn't know your name, nor Rachel's, until the meeting today. I just knew that a Columbine parent was coming to speak about his daughter. But 3 nights ago, while I was reading from the Old Testament, I felt a strong urge that I was supposed to have whoever was coming to speak to read this passage from Jeremiah. I didn't know why then - - but I do now!"*

She handed me her Bible which was opened to Jeremiah chapter 31. Jeremiah was called the "weeping prophet." She told me to start reading at verse 15: *"This is what the Lord says, 'A voice is heard in Ramah, mourning and great weeping, Rachel weeping for her children and refusing to be comforted because they are no more."*

"This is what the Lords says, 'Restrain your voice from weeping and your eyes from tears, for your work will be rewarded. They will return from the land of the enemy. So, there is hope for your descendants. Your children will return to their own land."

I was just as stunned as when I first saw Rachel's drawing! Those words from Jeremiah went right into my spirit and I knew, without a shadow of a doubt that Rachel's death had not been in vain. In fact, shortly after that I wrote these words on her memorial cross:

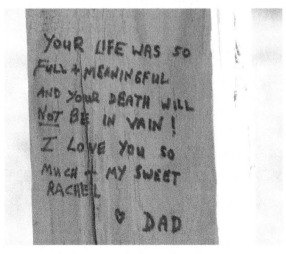

That passage from Jeremiah was so important that it was repeated by Luke in the New Testament. That prophecy was fulfilled when Jesus was just a baby. King Herod heard from the wise men that a king had been born in Bethlehem, and in a jealous fit of rage he ordered every baby boy under the age of 2 around Bethlehem to be slaughtered.

I knew that Jeremiah wasn't prophesying about my daughter, but those words were somehow meant for me that day in Jackson, Tennessee.

Even as Jeremiah prophesied, our work has been rewarded. Rachel's story has helped deliver millions of young people from the prison of depression and the clutches of suicide. They have returned from the land of captivity back to the land of freedom!

Here are just a few examples of letters we receive from young people who were planning to take their lives. We don't edit or change the spelling on the letters and emails they send to us:

> Rachel's impact on me was that I decided not to pull my trigger. The day you came to my school. I was planing on committing sucide.
> then, Dave told us to close our eyes and think about every one that we care about most..
>
> see I was in foster care and then my aunt said she would take me and my sister, but i did something wrong (i dont know what i did though) and she said she didnt want me anymore, and because of that my sister doesnt talk to me. she barely looks at me. any ways. when I closed my eyes. I saw my sister looking at me. smiling, loving, and i know now that if I would have went to the place where Im staying and commited sucide. I would
> never get to see that smiling face EVER again. So thank you, for telling me about Rachel's challenge, you saved a life
>
> *E. New York*

The day you came to visit my school, only a few hours before the presentation i had thought about committing suicide that evening. i felt invisible to my classmates and family. thought there was no reason in life. then i sat through the program and realized that there are kids like racheal. that didnt get a choice in living. i ended telling my family
everything and now i am getting help for my problems. i have also made my impact on the world by being nicer and donating my free time to different causes.

C. Texas

I didn't think much of Rachel's story before it was actually presented. About three days before, I actually very strongly considering suicide. I used to cause self inflicting pain on myself. I started deciding it wasn't enough after a while, and, I felt that once I died, I would be at peace. Therefore, I wanted to start planning my death. I knew where to get the pills, so I was trying to get some money for them...

Once I heard about Rachel's story, I comepletely dropped the suicide idea. I didn't want that anymore. All I want to do now is help people. People in need, that feel sad, or broken, or helpless, lost, ore even crazy. I've felt all of those, so I know what it's like, to be, the outcast, the bullied one, the crazy one, the broken kid that keeps to herself because she's to afraid to reach out anymore.

Rachel's Challenge has made me want to help, and that has become my life goal. I am so thankful for Rachel. Just hearing her story, and
thoughts...has saved my life. So, yes. I accept Rachel's Challenge. It seems like one of the best ideas to make an impact on the world.

L. Montana

i come from Africa(Botswana). people always make fun of my accent and words that i dont pronounce right!They even make fun of my name. I dont really have any friends, people i talk to always talk about me behind my back! when you came to my school and talked about the Rachel's challenge people sarted being nice to me. That saved my life because every once in a while i think about comitting suicide. Thanks for coming to my school! you saved my life. Thanks to Rachel

T. Michigan

Rachel's story saved my life.. I knew i was heading down the wrong path, and I would often let out anger on others I care about. I was planning for a long time to kill myself.. and my desicion still wasn't final until today..
I decided not to..

Rachel helped me see how much life there is and how I personally can start a chain reaction..so that is exactly what im doing.
I'm accepting Rachel's challenge.

New York

I first heard rachels challenge when i was in the 8th grade at an assembly & it touch me very deeply. Before i heard of this challenge i had thought about killing myself. I had alot going on at the time and i felt like nothing in my life was going right so i had no reason or point in being here. The stress and depression i was going threw had gotten to me badly and so i decided that i was going to commit suicide. But then i heard rachels challenge.

Noone knows how Rachel inspired & changed my life .. if it wasnt for Rachels challenge i wouldnt be here right now. She had such an impact on my life. Rahcels love & compasion for people has gone along way it has made me change my life and think right.

A. Ohio

72

Rachel's challenge really saved me as a student. today we had a presentation about Rachel and her dreams. it really impacted my self and others. it was last year In 6th grade. I was planning on killing myself, because I felt like no one understood me, and that no one cared.

I planed on over dosing on my migraine medicine. thank go d I didn't because I would've never got t hear about Rachel. it real- ly made me think about who I am and was. it was the last month
before school let out, I was bullying this girl because she didn't have the designer clothing well it got to the point she almost killed her self. after I talked and apologized, I understood that her father lost his job...during the presentation where the young man that was physically disabled and he said he wanted to kill hermself because of bullying, I lost it. I came up ther crying and said "I love you. I never want to loose you."

Rachel died with her goals and saying that she would change the world, they did! i m**** b***** declare this day the day i change the way i look, think and speak to one another. Rachel wanted her goals to live on after her death, well i, my self will make sure that her goals live on. i accept Rachel's challenge.

M.

These are just a few examples of the hundreds of heart-wrenching stories that flood into our office every year. The tears that Rachel drew have become seeds of hope to so many! We also know of 8 school shootings that were prevented because of students hearing Rachels story.

One of the stories I heard personally was from a young girl in high school in Texas. Here name is Hope - - but she had given up on hope for her life. Listen to her incredible story through this QR code:

73

Chapter 7
THE DAY RACHEL DIED

April 20, 1999 was one of the first warm days of spring in Colorado. Rachel and her brother, Craig, got in her red Acura Legend and headed for Columbine High School. Rachel was a junior and Craig was a freshman. Rachel turned on the radio to listen to her favorite station, but Craig kept changing it to another station.

Rachel was pretty upset with Craig, and they got into a big argument before they reached the school. Craig got out of the car - - slammed the door - - and never looked back. It would be the last time he would ever see his sister alive. He would look back with regret many times in the future at those final moments with Rachel.

All we know about her first 3 classes was that she started drawing the picture of her eyes and tears in her math class. After completing the picture in Mrs. Caruthers class, she headed out for lunch, but on the way, she went into the girls' restroom.

Another girl was standing in front of the restroom mirror trying to get something out of her eye, when Rachel walked in. Her name was Lindsey.

Lindsey would later tell me that when Rachel came into the restroom, she saw that Lindsey was picking at her eye and she asked if she was okay.

Lindsay said that Rachel looked somewhat pale, and she said to Lindsey, *"I just have a strange felling about today."* Lindsey didn't think much of it at the time, but later it would hit her that Rachel may have been sensing the rolling thunder of evil that was about to unleash itself on the students at Columbine.

Rachel went from there to the cafeteria, picked up her lunch, and headed out to the west entrance at the back of the school to join her friend, Richard Castaldo, for lunch.

Rachel and Richard sat down on the grass near the glass entry doors enjoying the warm sunshine and the beautiful view of the mountains in the distance.

Suddenly, without warning, two boys wearing black duster coats came over the small hill behind the school and opened fire. They sprayed bullets all over the glass doors, hitting both Rachel and Richard multiple times with random shots.

As the boys approached them, Rachel recognized Eric Harris and Dylan Klebold, students that she had shared a class with. Eric approached Rachel with his nine-millimeter - - lifted her head by her hair - - and asked in a mocking tone: *"Do you still believe in God?"*

Rachel looked at him through her pain and replied, *"You know I do!"* Eric sneered and said, *"Then go be with him"*, and he shot my daughter in the head.

75

The reason we know what happened is because Richard Castaldo's mom told us that Richard told her all this in the hospital before he went into a coma. Unfortunately, Richard would be paralyzed from the waist down and be confined to a wheelchair for the rest of his life.

After he came out of the coma, Richard could not remember what had happened, but his mom insisted that he had told her the whole story before he passed out.

Dateline MSNBC did an hour-long program about Rachel with our family, and they pointed out that many people doubted Richard's story, since his memory had failed after the coma. My son, Craig, was with me when I picked up the phone and called Richard's mom, and she confirmed the whole thing to the folks at Dateline.

To hear the phone call with Richard's mom:

Dave Cullen, who I met briefly, wrote a bestseller titled, _Columbine_, which became the "official" story of the Columbine tragedy. In it, he barely mentioned Rachel, but he wrote that she _"died instantly"_, killed in a hail of bullets, and she never was asked about God, much less that she replied, _"You know I do."_

I purchased the book and was amazed at the errors he made concerning Rachel. Not only was he wrong about her dying instantly, but he wrote that she was the "_senior class sweetheart_" (pg. 8 of his book).

To his credit, after I corrected him about it, he changed it to _"junior class sweetheart"_ in a revised edition. However, he did not change the error that she died instantly. And to my knowledge, Rachel was never referred to as the "junior class sweetheart" by anyone but Dave Cullen. (I'm not sure where he got that from). After living through that horrible tragedy, I have learned to always question the media!

76

Dave never interviewed our family, and to my knowledge he never interviewed Richard Castaldo or any of the other victims' families. A lot of his references seemed to come from newspaper articles at the time, many of which contained erroneous information.

Our verification of what happened came directly from both Richard and his mom. My friend, David Barton, taught me a long time ago to go to original sources - - not hearsay.

**RACHEL
and
MIKE
SCOTT**

In my live presentation, I never focused much on Rachel's last words. I didn't need to. Her life and writings gave ample proof of her faith. But Rachel was not the only victim in our family. My son, Craig was a freshman at Columbine and was in the library, which became the killing zone, when the shooting started.

Craig, along with his two friends, Matthew Kechter and Isaiah Sheols, were sitting at a table, quietly talking about football. Matt and Isaiah were both on the football team. Suddenly they heard what they thought were firecrackers outside the school.

They thought that it was probably a senior prank, since it was nearing graduation time and the seniors had talked about doing some harmless mischief before they graduated.

Craig would later reflect back on what he thought were firecrackers and realize that they were the sounds of bullets that were taking the life of his sister and wounding Richard Castaldo.

But suddenly the door to the library burst open and a student who had been shot stumbled into the room, covered in blood!

A part-time teacher, Pattie Nielson, rushed into the room and immediately yelled for students to get under their desks for protection. Pattie had already been wounded by shrapnel and she called 911.

Just a few seconds later, the two shooters entered the library and opened fire. Craig and his friends huddled together under a table, hoping against hope that the killers would not come over to where they were.

Isaiah, who was one of the few black students at Columbine, immediately became a target for the shooters. They began to taunt Isaiah unmercifully with racial slurs, using the "N" word and revealing their deep racial prejudice. Then they shot and killed Isaiah and Matt.

My son lay under that table, covered in the blood of his 2 friends and played dead. I can't imagine the fear that was flooding Craig's mind, believing that he would be the next victim. But a second before they pulled the trigger the alarm went off from gun smoke in the room.

The alarm distracted Eric and Dylan and they never came back to Craig's location, or I would have lost 2 of my children that day. I still shudder at the thought of how close Craig came to dying.

After the shooters left the room and the smoke began to clear, ten innocent, precious children lay dead, and a dozen others were wounded.

Craig got up off the floor from between the bodies of his 2 friends and began yelling for everyone to get out of the library. Fortunately, most of them did, because 24 minutes later, the killers came back to the library where they would commit suicide. Two students and a teacher that had been injured and left for dead were still in the room.

CRAIG & DARRELL YEARS AFTER THE TRAGEDY

Craig heard a girl named Kacey begging for help. Kacey's shoulder had been hit by a shotgun blast and was shredded. She almost lost that arm, but doctors were able to patch it back up.

Craig helped Kacey get out of the library, and as they exited the building at the back entrance, Craig walked past the body of his sister, Rachel, not realizing who it was.

As I write this, I can still feel the horror of that day and the terrible ordeal that Craig went through. Losing my daughter, and coming within seconds of losing my son, was almost more than I could bear.

So, let me tell you where I was when I heard the news about what was happening. I had gone to an antique shopping center that morning where I had a seller's booth.

I was putting a few antiques on the shelves when my cell phone rang. It was my fiancé, Sandy, who would soon become my wife.

SANDY AND RACHEL

Sandy told me, in a panicked voice, that there had been a shooting at Columbine. She didn't know much more than that because the news had just been released.

I rushed out to my truck and headed over to the school with my heart pounding in my chest. I turned on the radio, and what I heard nearly gave me a heart attack! The radio announcer was crying and saying that dozens of students had been shot and many of them had been killed.

I had 2 children at Columbine and my brother, Larry, did as well. Jeff and Sarah Scott, Rachel's cousins, were fortunately in safe zones and did not encounter the shooters. Although Jeff was in a locked room and saw Eric Harris try to open the door before moving on.

I got caught up in a massive traffic jam as I got near the school, as parents, family members, and concerned people tried to get over to Columbine. The radio announcer said that they were bussing survivors over to Leawood Elementary School, so I drove in that direction.

The first person I saw was my brother, Larry, who assured me that his children and Craig were all accounted for, but no one had heard from Rachel.

Sandy came to join me, and we frantically looked for Rachel to get off one of those buses that were bringing the students over from Columbine.

Rachel's mom and Stepdad, Beth, and Larry Nimmo, had gone to another location where they were also sending survivors. Sandy and I stayed in contact with them in case any of them heard anything about Rachel.

I ran out to where the buses were pulling in and stood on a fence to get a better view of students before they even got off the bus. At one point, I thought I saw Rachel through a bus window, but it turned out to be a girl that resembled her.

Darrell standing on fence:

When the last bus had pulled up and the last surviving students got off that bus at Leawood Elementary, our hopes began to dim. We began to speculate that maybe she was still in hiding somewhere in the school, or that she had been wounded and was in a hospital. Lists of survivors' names were posted on the wall, and we read, and reread those names, hoping to see Rachel's - - but never did.

We frantically called every hospital, but no Rachel Scott had been admitted.

81

It's a very sad situation when the best you can hope for is that your child has been shot and wounded and is in a hospital somewhere.

As the day drug on our hopes began to diminish. More and more parents were being united with their children, and by four o'clock that evening we were one of a small handful of families left.

We knew when they started asking about what clothes Rachel wore that day, that she was probably one of the victims. We did not get official word until noon the next day. Not knowing is one of the hardest things to deal with.

After a sleepless night, I went over to the Nimmo's house where Craig was, and he and I went out and sat on the curb. I was so pre-occupied with Rachel that I hadn't given much thought to Craig. He had, obviously, not been wounded, but he had not said much at all, and I wanted to help him open up about the tragedy.

I asked him casually what part of the school he was in when the shooting started, and when he told me I was stunned! He said, *"Dad, I was in the library - - the killing zone"*, and he began to cry as he informed me that he had lost 2 of his friends beside him.

I sat there in shock for several minutes, not able to even speak.

I suddenly realized that I didn't just lose a daughter, but that I came within seconds of losing a son also! We had 2 victims in our family! Craig was not physically wounded, but he was deeply wounded psychologically by what happened. No other student at Columbine lost a sibling who also lost two friends beside them on that day.

Craig not only had to deal with the horror of losing two friends. He also knew that he had come with a second or two of dying, as well. But the hardest thing for him to do was to forgive himself for getting into a fight with Rachel on the way to school that day.

82

His last memory of slamming the door on her and not looking back would haunt him for years to come.

Columbine was the first mass shooting in our nation's history. There had been random shootings in schools before Columbine, but usually the death count was 1 to 3 students. Most of those killings came from personal fights, anger at a teacher, a romance gone sour, etc.

The worst K-12 school shooting before Columbine occurred on January 17, 1989 in Cleveland Elementary School in Stockton, California. 5 students and the shooter died.

On May 1, 1997, a teacher and 3 students were killed in Oliverhust, California at Lindhurst High School.

In 1997 both Pearl, Mississippi and West Paduch, Kentucky experienced 3 shooting deaths each. Years after Columbine I would speak to all the students in both of those schools.

On March 28, 1998, a teacher and 4 students were killed at Westside Middle School in Craighead County, Arkansas.

But the world was overwhelmingly shocked by the massacre of a teacher and 12 students at Columbine. The two shooters committed suicide at the school, bringing the total to 15 dead!

But the toll did not stop there. Three Columbine students and a mom of one of the injured students all committed suicide shortly after the tragedy.

Here's a little-known fact about Rachel. If she had survived Columbine, she would probably have died 10 months later at the Subway sandwich shop she worked at after school and on weekends.

On the night before Valentine's Day, February 13, 2000, Stephanie Hart-Grizzell drove to that Subway sandwich shop to wait for her boyfriend, Nick Kunselman, to finish his shift. They were both students at Columbine and Nick had taken Rachel's job after she was killed.

Just after midnight another employee happened to drive by and noticed that the lights were still on, so he stopped to investigate. He found the door unlocked and bodies of Nick and Stephanee riddled with bullets. They never caught the shooter.

Stephanee was a friend of Rachel, and her bedroom window was just across the fence from Rachel's bedroom. The Subway shooting got a bit of local news exposure and soon was forgotten. If Rachel had died there, instead of Columbine, the world would have never known about her.

SUBWAY WHERE RACHEL WORKED

I have had many parents who have lost a child, or children, contact me and ask how I got through all the pain and sorrow. They wanted to know how to proceed.

My advice has always been simple. I encourage them to allow grief to run its course. Ecclesiastes 3:4-5 says, *"there is a time to weep and a time to laugh, a time to mourn and a time to dance."* I assure them that the day will come when they can laugh and dance again, but the time of weeping and mourning must be embraced first.

MY DAUGHTER, BETHANEE AND I, READING CARDS SENT TO OUR FAMILY AFTER THE TRAGEDY

The last thing I wanted to hear right after Rachel died was someone quoting the scripture at me that, *"all things work together for the good of those who love God and are called according to his purpose."* And yet, a few did. Even though I believe that verse, when it was quoted to me during that time, I just wanted to throw up!

85

All things did work together for good, but the timing had to be right. As we look back at all the incredible things that have happened - - at all the suicides that have been prevented - - at all the lives that have been changed - - we believe that Rachel would be pleased that her life counted!

Listen to my daughters, Bethanee, and Dana, as they talk about losing their sister. This was recorded shortly after Rachel died.

I also tell parents who have lost their children about Norman Grubb's input to our family - - to be see-throughers and not look-atters. I encourage them to remember the good times and celebrate their child's life. Don't focus on how they died. Focus on how they lived.

King David wrote: *"Thou hast turned my mourning into dancing for me; thou hast put off my sackcloth."*

Chapter 8
HER FUNERAL AND MEMORIAL SERVICES

The week following the Columbine shootings and Rachel's death were just a blur. The national and local media followed us everywhere we went.

Just 2 days after the tragedy, Katie Couric asked to do an interview with my son, Craig. I went with Craig to the park near the school to meet up with Katie. It was a cold snowy day, and the interview was to be outside. Katie had also asked Isaiah Shoel's stepdad to participate. Isaiah was one of the two of Craig's friends who was killed beside him in the library.

As Katie asked them about the racial slurs that were used against Isaiah before he was killed, suddenly Michael Shoels reached out and grasped Craig's hand. It was a memorable, pungent moment that would stay with me, and the watching television audience, forever.

In the years that followed, when I was speaking at a conference, inevitably, someone would bring up that moment and tell me how much they were impacted by it.

It was symbolic gesture that spoke volumes concerning how we should treat each other. It challenged the racial divide and prejudice that still exists in our nation. To see that powerfully impacting video click on the QR code below and watch the whole thing.

When Katie Couric retired from the Today Show, she reflected back on the most powerful interviews that she had during her long and successful career. Craig was invited to be a guest at her farewell broadcast, as she relived that interview from years earlier. She would say that it was one of the most spiritual experiences of her life.

The day after that interview between Craig, Michael Shoels, and Katie Couric, Sandy and I were at Olinger's Funeral Home selecting a casket for Rachel. We made the decision to have her buried in a white casket.

We knew that the school yearbooks had just come out, and she had been excited about having her friends sign hers. Since that couldn't happen, we chose a white casket so that her friends could sign it.

This had never been done before, and we had no idea that it was going to start a trend for parents who would bury their children.

By the time her funeral took place, a lot of her friends and family members had covered her casket with their names and their farewell statements to her. Below are some of her friends signing her casket. At the bottom right is one of her favorite teachers, Paula Reed.

I simply wrote on her casket, "I love you forever, Dad." Numerous national magazines featured pictures of her coffin. Today, if you Google the caskets of young people, you will find many of them that resemble Rachel's. They are written on and signed by those who knew and loved them.

There were so many funerals taking place that week! Rachel's took place at Trinity Christian Center, about a mile away from the school. We expected a few hundred people to be there, but we were stunned when over 3,000 showed up.

CNN asked for permission to film her entire funeral and it became the largest viewing audience in their history. More viewers watched Rachel's funeral on CNN than watched Princess Diana's. You can still view Rachel's entire funeral online.

Sandy and I, along with Rachel's mom and stepdad, were taken back to the pastor's office before the funeral began. Our children were there with us in the small room, along with a small group of friends. Everyone in the room knew each other and the atmosphere was very somber.

Police officers were posted at the door so that no one else could enter the room.

There was a small couch up against the wall that Sandy and I sat on as we waited for the funeral to begin. While we were sitting there, an elderly gentleman in a pinstripe suit came over and sat down on the couch next to me. He put his hand on my left knee and said, *"They were after her - - but it's going to be okay."* He said it in a very quiet but firm voice, then got up and walked away.

Sandy turned to me and asked, *"Who was that?"* Then it dawned on me that I knew everyone in the room - - but I had never seen this person before in my life!

I immediately got up and walked over to Beth, Rachel's mom, and asked her who he was. I said, *"Beth, who is the elderly man in the pinstriped suit?"* She looked around the room and said, *"What elderly man in a pinstriped suit?"* Sandy and I were both puzzled because he wasn't there.

I went over and asked one of the police officers if anyone had come in or exited the room and he said, *"No."*

Right then the pastor came in to take us all into the auditorium and I put the whole thing out of my mind until later.

Rachel's funeral was a mixture of extreme grief and a small insertion of joy. One of the speakers asked if any of Rachel's friends would like to say a few words - - and a swarm of young people flooded the platform. We listened, along with the rest of the world, as they shared story after story about Rachel's kindness and compassion to others.

Click on the QR code below and watch Rachel's youth leader, Lori, talking about Rachel at the funeral.

As the years have gone by, many people have come up to me in schools, churches, and conventions where I was speaking, and told me that they had watched Rachel's funeral on CNN that day.

An executive from CNN told me that more people watched Rachel's funeral on their network than had watched the funeral of Princess Diana.

Rachel parked her car a block from the school at Clement Park on the day of the tragedy. Her car, and a truck, belonging to another victim, John Tomlin, became massive memorials as people came from around the world and covered both vehicles with notes, teddy bears, and gifts.

One of those people, a man from Texas, sat near her car and wrote in his journal.

John Tomlin's truck   **Friends discover Rachel's car**

Eventually her car would be completely covered

The man sitting near Rachel's car, writing in his journal, was Paul Jackson. Paul was the executive director for Josh McDowell Ministries and had previously been the manager for a Christian rock group called, Petra. Before that he had managed the Oak Ridge Boys for years.

He wrote in his journal that he felt that somehow his life would be involved in the aftermath of this tragedy. He had no way of knowing that within a year he would be working with *Rachel's Challenge.*

Rachel was buried at Chapel Hill Memorial Gardens. The owners donated plots for Rachel and Corey DePooter, who also had been killed at Columbine. The brave teacher, Dave Sanders is also buried there.

Sandy and I have our burial plots right beside Rachel, so someday if you visit Rachel's grave, you may also see ours (hopefully not for a long time). Other family members also have burial plots at the same location.

A man by the name of Greg Zanis, had made 15 wooden crosses and placed them on a hill behind Columbine. It caused a lot of controversy because he included 2 crosses for the killers. Thousands of people from around the world made a pilgrimage to that location to view, and often write things on the crosses.

CROSSES ON THE HILL ABOVE COLUMBINE

Greg would later carry 13 of those crosses, representing the victims, to events where I was speaking. He became famous for building and delivering crosses and stars of David to funerals and memorials.

92

Greg delivered over 26,000 crosses in the years following Columbine until his death on May 4, 2020 - - my birthday. He founded an organization called, *"Crosses for Losses."* He was an eccentric, but lovable man. I miss him. His 13 crosses would eventually end up at Rachel's gravesite as a memorial to all the victims of Columbine.

People came from around the world to visit Rachel's grave and the 13 crosses representing the teacher and 12 students who were killed.

The wooden crosses were eventually replaced with marble ones:

The very next day, after Rachel's funeral, there was a massive memorial service for all the Columbine victims. 65,000 people attended the event which was at a theater parking lot.

Sandy and I were escorted to the front, along with all the victim's families, where we were greeted by Vice-President Gore and General Colin Powell, who would go on to be Secretary of State.

Suddenly, Michael W. Smith came out of the theater and headed straight for Sandy and I. We were surprised when he took us backstage into one of the theater rooms where we were joined by Amy Grant. Amy and Michael were brought in to sing at the memorial service. They had both heard about Rachel and seen her funeral the day before, and they wanted to help comfort us.

Amy had her acoustic guitar, and she began to play and sing, *I Surrender All*. It was a sacred moment. Amy, Michael, Sandy, and I quietly wept at this beautiful tribute to Rachel. Michael W. Smith later wrote about it in his book, *This Is Your Time*.

From time to time our paths would cross at different events with Michael. We will always be grateful for what he and Amy Grant did that day.

Here is what Michael wrote about our first encounter, in his book, *This Is Your Time.*

THIS IS YOUR TIME

One of the gunmen walked over to Rachel, who was now facedown on the ground but still alive, and picked up her head by her hair.

"Do you still believe in God?" he asked.

With tremendous courage, Rachel used what little life she had left to whisper, "You know that I do."

A second later, Rachel was immediately with the Lord.

At the theater, Rachel's dad, Darrell Scott, hugged me and said, "Rachel loved your music."

I'm still surprised when people tell me this, but in this context, I was almost knocked over. For some reason, I felt an immediate connection with Rachel and grieved the loss of her life, even though I had never met her.

All this added to the surreal feeling that shrouded the entire day.

"I'm so sorry," I told him, again not realizing the awesome things that God had planned for Rachel's dad. Darrell would eventually travel across the country, speaking words of grace and hope to many. Rachel's death created a powerful ministry of evangelism and challenge to the Church. Darrell often reads from Rachel's diary when he speaks, and virtually everywhere he goes, a hundred or more kids come up and commit or recommit their hearts to the Lord.

DOING THE DAVID THING

After Rachel's dad spoke, it got eerily quiet, creating a real awkward situation. Then Amy did something brilliant. She walked over to her guitar, picked it up, and started quietly singing a hymn, "I Surrender All."

One by one, we were all mesmerized. Something almost mystical happened when she started to sing. The grief never left, but it was covered with a grace and assurance that took away some of the sting.

Michael had written a song, also called, *This Is Your Time*, which he initially dedicated to Cassie Bernall, another Columbine victim. He later rededicated it to both Rachel and Cassie.

Exactly one year after the tragedy, on April 20, 2000, Paul Jackson and Josh McDowell would host a memorial service that honored all the victims, but specifically focused on Rachel and the new organization that Sandy and I had created called, *Columbine Redemption*.

I had been speaking in large arena events in the year following the tragedy under the *Columbine Redemption* umbrella, and the one-year memorial event was put together by Paul, Josh, and I.

Michael W. Smith sang at the event, as well as Pillips, Craig, and Dean. Randy Phillips was the lead singer for the trio, and I knew his dad and mom well. Kenneth and Wanda Phillips were a couple that had impacted my life at an early age. I was honored to be invited by Kenneth to speak at his church in Austin, Texas a short time after that memorial service.

Martin Luther King III, the son of legendary Martin Luther King, Jr., attended the Columbine Redemption event, and we invited him to greet the audience.

In the years to come, I would share the podium with all of Dr. King's children.

My daughter, Dana, performed a powerful mime at the memorial event. Rachel had taught her the mime just a few days before she was killed. It was called, *Watch the Lamb*. Rachel had performed it at her high school talent show just a few weeks before she died at Columbine. Sandy and I attended and brought roses for her at the end of the show.

The music tape messed up while Rachel was performing at her high school talent show, but the young man running the sound equipment quickly corrected it. Ironically, that young man was Dylan Klebold, one of the killers at Columbine.

To see the end of the mime performed by a young lady at Rachel's funeral, see the QR code:

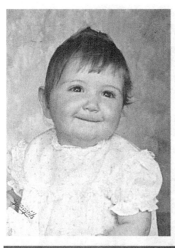

Chapter 9
SHADOWS AND PREMONITIONS

I am aware that this chapter will be harshly criticized by some, but I felt that it needed to be written. Throughout history, there have been "types and shadows" of events from the past or the future. Some call them prophetic and some say that they are just co-incidents.

For example, the Titanic, which sank on April 14, 1912, was a historic event that everyone is aware of. What some people don't know is that a book published in 1885, fourteen years before the Titanic sank, eerily described what would happen. The book's title was originally *"Futility"*, but was later changed to, *"The Wreck of the Titan."*

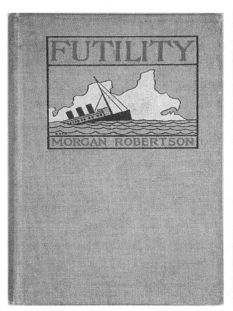
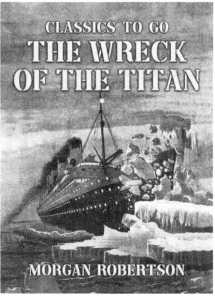

The book was about the largest, fastest new ship in the world. It was called the Titan. While sailing between Ireland and America it hits an iceberg on the starboard side, at midnight, with a shortage of lifeboats and the survivors are rescued by a nearby ship. *(Sound familiar?)*

The Titan was 800 feet long
The Titanic was 882 feet long

The Titan's speed was 25 knots.
The Titanic's speed was 22.5 knots.

The Titan had 2,500 passengers.
The Titanic had 2,200 passengers.

The Titan was declared to be "unsinkable".
The Titanic was declared to be "unsinkable".

The Titan was British owned.
The Titanic was British owned.

The Titan was hit by an iceberg.
The Titanic was hit by an iceberg.

The Titan was hit by an iceberg at midnight.
The Titanic was hit by an iceberg at midnight.

The Titan was hit on the starboard side.
The Titanic was hit on the starboard side.

The Titan sank in the North Atlantic exactly 400 nautical miles from Newfoundland.
The Titanic sank in the North Atlantic exactly 400 nautical miles from Newfoundland.

The Titan had a triple screw propeller.
The Titanic had a triple screw propeller.

The Titan had a severe lack of lifeboats.
The Titanic had a severe lack of lifeboats.

The Titan and the Titanic both chose the same route between America and Ireland.

Many people who read the book, *The Wreck of the Titan,* saw it as a premonition of what would actually happen 14 years later.

Another amazing "type and shadow" is the similarities between the deaths of Presidents Abraham Lincoln and John F. Kennedy.

Lincoln was elected to Congress in 1846.
JFK was elected to Congress in 1946.

Lincoln was elected President in 1860.
JFK was elected President in 1960.

Lincoln lost a child while living in the White House.
JFK lost a child while living in the White House.

Lincoln was a civil rights President.
JFK was a civil rights President.

Lincoln's secretary, Kennedy, told him not to go to the theater.
Kennedy's secretary, Lincoln, told him not to go to Dallas.

Lincoln was shot in the back of his head.
JFK was shot in the back of his head.

Lincoln was shot on Friday.
JFK was shot on Friday.

Lincoln's assassin, John Wilkes Booth, was known by 3 names consisting of 15 letters.
JFK's assassin, Lee Harvey Oswald, was known by 3 names consisting of 15 letters.

Booth shot Lincoln in a theater and ran to a warehouse.
Oswald shot JFK from a warehouse and ran to a theater.

Booth was killed before he could be put on trial.
Oswald was killed before he could be put on trial.

There were conspiracy theories around Lincoln's death.
There were conspiracy theories around JFK's death.

Lincoln's successor was VP Johnson.
JFK's successor was VP Johnson.

Andrew Johnson was born in 1808.
Lyndon Johnson was born in 1908.

Andrew Johnson died 10 years after Lincoln's death.
Lyndon Johnson died 10 years after JFK's death.

In 1861 a NY police officer uncovered a plot to assassinate Lincoln.
His name was - - - John Kennedy!

Perhaps all of this is just co-incidence - - *but really?* As we look at the similarities between Columbine and the events surrounding Calvary, I will leave it up to you to decide. However, the facts presented are real.

The word, "Columbine" means *"like a dove."* The Columbine flower is dove-like in appearance. This the same description that John the Baptist gave when the Holy Spirit descended on Jesus at his baptism. It descended *"like a dove".*

At Columbine a teacher and 12 students would impact the world
Jesus, the great teacher, and his 12 disciples would impact the world.

The first teacher was called *"the Son of David."*
The teacher killed at Columbine was named David.

Jesus was called *"the Lamb of God."*
Rachel's name in Hebrew means *"little lamb."*

More than half of the Columbine victims had Biblical names: Rachel,
2 Daniels, Matthew, John, Isaiah, David and Steven.

The "Son of David" willingly died to save the world.
David Sanders willingly gave his life to save his students.

At the birth of Jesus, angels *(messengers)* brought "good tidings of
great joy to all the people."
Before Rachel's birth a messenger (Lattie McDonough) said, *"She
will bring joy to the hearts of many people."*

Jesus predicted that he would be killed.
Rachel predicted that she would be killed. *(You'll see this later)*

Prophets had dreams and visions of things Jesus would do.
Frank Amedia had a repetitive dream of Rachel's drawing.

Jesus' final words before he died were, *"It is finished."*
Some of Rachel's final words were, *"It isn't finished."*
The picture was finished, but the impact from her life wasn't.

An angel appeared at Jesus' tomb to let his disciples know that it
everything would be okay.
An angel *(elderly gentleman)* appeared at Rachel's funeral to assure
us that everything was going to be okay.

Remember - - that old man *(angel)* told me that they were after her.
That was confirmed by both Richard Castaldo and the killers
themselves.

They recorded themselves on video talking about killing Rachel and
another student.

Matt Lauer played that tape on the Today Show in an interview that he and I did. See QR code:

There are other things that happened around the events of the tragedy that seemed spiritual in nature. Some of them are documented, while some are subjective and cannot be proven.

For example, after Sandy called and told me about the shootings taking place, I rushed out to my truck and headed for the school. I kept hearing, in my mind, the words, *"This is a spiritual event,"* over and over. It wasn't audible, but it was very real.

This was before I knew that we had lost Rachel. When I got to Leawood Elementary School where they were instructing us to go on the radio, the first person I saw was my brother, Larry. The first thing I said to him was, *"Larry, this is a spiritual event."*

Now, can I prove that I heard a voice in my head? NO. But many people who heard me say it can verify what I told them.

Another thing that I can't prove is that a lady I ran into at a grocery store, who had seen me on tv, told me that early in the morning of April 20, she was driving to work and as she drove near the school, she felt compelled to pull into the Columbine parking lot and pray.

She said that she had an overwhelming sense of sadness and that she broke down and cried while she prayed for the students at the school. She said that after a few minutes, the burden lifted, and she felt a sense of relief. I wish I had taken her name and phone number, but I didn't.

Some might say, *"What was that all about? The tragedy happened despite her prayer!"* And they would be right.

But - - - it is a fact, according to police reports, that over 500 people would have died that day if the two 20-pound propane tanks had exploded that Eric and Dylan placed in the cafeteria. I'm not saying that this lady's prayer prevented anything. I'm simply writing about what she told me.

Can I prove that an angel sat down next to me at Rachel's funeral and assured me that everything was going to be okay? No - - - but I know, without a doubt that it happened. I am so glad that Sandy saw and heard that old man in the pinstripe suit.

There are some things that cannot be explained. There are some things that cannot be proven. But that doesn't mean that they are not true.

Sometimes we feel things that we can never express with words. There's an *"old saying"* that says, *"It's better felt than telt."* I wrote a poem by that title in my book, *Thirsty Fish*.

FELT or TELT?

It's better felt than telt - - it's better touched or smelt
Then all the knowledge you acquire or dogmas you have helt

Experience, not knowledge, awakens us within
So joy and peace can now increase, and purpose can ascend

Awareness opens fountains, that thinking never will
The streams abide, down deep inside, until your mind is still

Awakening to purpose - - aware of here and now
With hearts aglow, we start to grow, as spirit shows us how

It's better felt than telt - - it's better touched and smelt
Then all the knowledge you acquire, or doctrines you have helt

Quantum physics is just now beginning to confirm what Hebrews 11:3 told us: *"Things that are seen are not made of things that do appear."* Rachel had premonitions about her death in the last year of her life. On April 20, 1998 - - exactly one year to the day before she died, she wrote in her diary, addressed to her friend Samantha:

April 20, 98

Dear Sam,

     It's like I have a heavy heart and this burden upon my back... but I don't know what it is. There is something in me that makes me want to cry... and I don't even know what it is. Things have definetly changed. Last week was so hard... besides missing Breakthru... I lost all of my friends at school. Now that I have begun to walk my talk, they make fun of me. I don't even know what I have done. I don't really have to say anything, and they turn me away.)

But you know what.... it's all worth it to me. I am not going to apoligize for speaking the Name of Jesus, I am not going to justify my faith to them, and I am not going to hide the light that God has put into me. If I have to sacrafice everything... I will. I will take it. If my friends have to become my enemies for me to be with my best friend Jesus, then that's fine with me.)

She started off by telling Samantha that she felt something within her that made her wasn't to cry, and she didn't know what it was.

The last sentence in that diary entry, written exactly one year to the day before she was killed, proclaims that she was willing to sacrifice everything.

Eleven months before she died she wrote:

May 2nd
This will be my last year Lord.
I have gotten what I can.
Thank you.

She talked with a number of her friends and confided in them that she would not live to be very old. They said that she never was morbid or depressed about it - - just matter of fact.

Listen to what her friends told us that Rachel said to them about dying young:

Her feelings concerning the shortness of her life seemed to intensify the closer she came to that final day, as this diary entry reflects:

I'm slowly dying,
Just a memory,
I'm slowly dying
There's nothing left of me.

107

In her writing below, she revealed for the first and only time, how she thought she would die - - as a homicide victim.

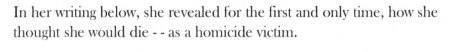

> I'm dying
>   quickly my soul leaves
>   slowly my body withers.
>
> It isn't suicide, I consider it
>   homicide. The world you
> have created has led to my
>   death.

I don't think Rachel was talking about God when she wrote, "The world you have created has led to my death." I think she was talking about us - - about the world, we as humans have created. A world of division, hatred, jealousy, pollution, and war! We, collectively, are the villains that created the world that led to her death - - but we can change that!

Here's another diary entry hinting that her life would be short:

> Just passing by
>
> Just coming thru
>
> Not staying long
>
> I always knew
>
> This home I have
>
> will never last

Her final poem was written just days before she died:

Am I the only one who sees
Am I the only one who craves your glory
Am I the only one who longs
To be in forever Your loving arms
All I want is for someone to walk with me
Through these halls of a tragedy
Please give me a loving friend
Who will carry your name, until the end
Someone who longs to be with you
Someone who will stay forever true

"Who will you give to walk with me through these halls of a tragedy?"
WOW! What was she feeling? What was she seeing? What was she
thinking when she wrote these words?

To conclude this chapter, here is a simple prayer that she prayed:

Father, reach out Your hand,
Grab a hold of my life.
Open my eyes,
To Your wonderful light.
Fill me up,
With Your undying love.
Save me a place,
In Your kingdom above.

~ by Rachel Joy Scott

Chapter 10
AUSTIN, AMBER, VAL, and MARK

AUSTIN

Several months after Rachel died I went out, as I often do, to her grave. As I approached, I saw a young man putting some fresh flowers there. I introduced myself and asked if he had been a friend of Rachel's. The story he told me is one that we now share with millions of young people in our school assemblies. Here it is:

Austin was driving home from work on a dark, rainy night and he was in a bad mood. He was a disc jockey at a local radio station and had made some mistakes that day, got yelled at, and was just not feeling very good.

Then, to make things worse, one of his tires went flat while driving home. He didn't have an umbrella and it was pouring down rain, but he knew he had to change his tire.

Right about then, a little red Acura Legend pulled up and a girl jumped out with an umbrella and said, *"Hi, I'm Rachel. Looks like you might need some help! So can I help you out?"* Austin told me that he was in such a bad mood, and Rachel was so cheerful, that at first she just irritated him!

But he said that within minutes his whole attitude changed. He was grateful that this young girl was willing to stand out in the rain and hold an umbrella over him while changed his tire. She kept him from getting soaked while he did the work.

When he finished, she turned to go, and Austin thanked her for taking the time to go out of her way to help him out. A few days later, Austin picked up the morning paper and was stunned to see Rachel's picture on the front page as one of Columbine's victims.

110

Austin went to Rachel's funeral, and as he walked by her casket, he made a vow to repay that act of kindness. He has taught his children to be kind and compassionate with Rachel as their role model. See Austin tell the story through the QR code:

But Rachel's impact on Austin and his family didn't stop at her funeral. Within several months, Austin and his wife had a newborn baby girl. Guess what they named her? His little Rachel will someday be a grandmother and she will be telling her grandchildren about a young girl, who many years ago, stopped and helped her dad fix a flat on a rainy night! And the legacy will continue.

AMBER

Amber was the new kid at school. Her dad had moved her and her brothers from Atlanta, Georgia to Littleton.

She didn't know anyone at Columbine, so at lunchtime she sat by herself in the cafeteria. Rachel was sitting with some of her friends nearby when she noticed that Amber looked sad.

Rachel got up, and carried her tray over to where Amber was sitting and asked if she could join her for lunch. She then went back and got her friends to join her at Amber's table.

Amber said that instantly, one of her worst days at school became one of her best, because of Rachel's kindness.

What Rachel, and no one else in the cafeteria knew, was that Amber's mom had died in a car accident just a month earlier.

Too often we fail to realize the struggles and heartbreak that others are going through. Rachel didn't just write: *"I have this theory that if one person will go out of their way to show compassion, it will start a chain reaction of the same. People will never know how far a little kindness will go."* She practiced the things she wrote about.

Rachel's Challenge partnered with an organization called, *The Foundation for a Better Life*, which put out a national television piece reflecting what Rachel did that day in reaching out to Amber. See QR code:

VAL

Valerie, known by her friends as Val, felt like an outsider at Columbine. She was a tough girl who had experimented with drugs and got into trouble at school for drug use. She said that people ignored her and no one wanted to talk with her, until she met Rachel.

Rachel accepted Val, and her friendship was unconditional. Rachel never asked any of her friends to change, and she never tried to "convert" anyone to her beliefs and lifestyle.

But, ironically, many of the people that Rachel encountered did change. Influence is the greatest form of persuasion. When we simply love and accept a person the way they are, they often end up changing for the better, without pressure or attempts to change them.

Val said, *"Rachel made me want to be a better person."* And that happened! What a powerful statement, *"She made me want to be a better person!"*

Val got off of drugs and shed her "tough girl" image and began to practice kindness toward others. Today she is a Christian believer and a friend of our family. See the QR code to hear Val talk about it:

Rachel's favorite Bible verse was Isaiah 50 verse 4: *"The Lord God has given me the tongue of the learned, that I should know how to speak a word in season to him that is weary."*

Many translations say, *"a disciplined tongue."* The *"tongue of the learned"* results in 4 distinct steps. The first is "know-how." All skilled musicians, athletes, speakers, etc. have developed "know-how" in order to be effective. There are many people who do not *know how* to approach others in order to bring them comfort or friendship.

Standing on a street corner and yelling at people to repent is not an example of someone with the "know-how" to change lives. In fact, none of us can change another person's life. Only God can do that, and the person must want to change.

Unconditional love is the key to helping others want to change. When Rachel reached out to help Austin fix a flat on that dark, rainy night, she did not try to change his bad mood. She had no other agenda except to show kindness to someone in need. But his mood changed because of her unconditional love and acceptance.

When she reached out to Amber, she was not trying to change Amber's sadness into happiness. But that's what happened. When we quit trying to change others - - our parents - - our spouse - - our friends - - our children - - and accept them unconditionally where they are - - miraculously, change often occurs!

When she reached out to Val, she was not trying to get her off drugs or soften up her "tough girl" image. Instead, like the old hymn says, *"just as I am, without one plea,"* Rachel accepted Val where she was, without trying to change her!

Some people may never change, but they will respond to unconditional love that isn't trying to change them, and accepts them just the way they are.

So, the first step in exercising a disciplined tongue is - - to learn! And the learning process produces *"know-how."* Many lives have been touched and changed because of Rachel's know-how.

The second step is to *"speak a word."* A word - - not just any word! And not a flood of words! Proverbs 27:11 says, *"A word fitly spoken is like apples of gold in settings of silver."* The right word can make all the difference in the world to a person who is hurting.

While we were waiting at Leawood Elementary School to find out whether Rachel was a victim or not, a well-meaning pastor came up to Sandy and I and realized that we were in great distress. He put his hand on my shoulder and said, *"Darrell, you know that God is in control and that everything works out for the good."*

Even though he meant well, I cringed, and both Sandy and I felt irritated.

His words were not *"apples of gold in settings of silver"* at that point in time. It was the wrong place, the wrong time, and the wrong words. In contrast that pastor's insensitivity, as we sat there anxiously waiting, we both felt a sense of comfort come over us.

I happened to turn around at that time, and behind us was a Catholic nun, with her head down, silently praying for Sandy and I.

Although I am not Catholic, I know that that dear lady was pouring out unconditional love toward us. Both Sandy and I turned around and embraced her and we all wept together. Her sensitivity to our situation allowed her to speak the right word, without saying a thing!

St. Francis of Assisi once said, *"Preach the gospel at all times, and if necessary use words."* He knew, just as Rachel did, that actions speak louder than words. In her Codes of Life, Rachel challenged us to *SHOW* compassion - - not just speak words of compassion.

114

The third element in developing a tongue of the learned is having the know-how to speak a word "*in season.*" As illustrated above, there is a right time and there is a wrong time to speak truth to others. We are told in scripture to "*speak the truth in love,*" but unfortunately many people speak the truth with a wrong attitude or wrong motives.

President Ronald Reagan was a man who was skilled in speaking the right word at the right time. He was running against Walter Mondale for the presidential office in 1984, and there was a lot of concern about his age (73) at that time.

He addressed the issue by saying, "*I am not going to exploit, for political purposes, my opponent's youth and inexperience.*" Even Mondale laughed with the crowd. Reagan won by a landslide.

And who can forget the perfect timing of his words to Russian President Gorbachev in Berlin when he said, "*Mr. Gorbachev, tear down this wall!*" President Reagan was a wordsmith. A man with a disciplined tongue who could speak a word, in season.

The fourth and last element from Isaiah 50:4 concerning a disciplined tongue is: "*to him that is weary.*" Too often people must become weary of the way they have lived before they want to change. They must hit rock bottom before they can even hear the truth that can set them free.

SISTERS: DANA, BETHANEE, RACHEL

Rachel had developed a "disciplined tongue" that knew how to speak a word, in season, those who were weary. That's why she wrote so often about "reaching the unreached." She was not talking about preaching at them - - she was talking about showing kindness, love and friendship.

RACHEL WITH HER DAD

Her sensitivity to others can be seen in her writing below:

> A friend...
> A friend is someone who can
> look into your eyes and be able
> to tell if your alright or not
> A friend...
> A friend is someone who can
> say something to you
> without you telling them
> anything and their words hit
> the spot
> A friend...
> A friend is someone who can
> brighten your day with a simple
> smile when others try to do it
> with a 1,000 words

She wrote, *"A friend is someone who can look into your eyes and be able to tell if you're alright or not."* That is the know-how in action!

Then she wrote, *"A friend is someone who can say something to you without you telling them anything, and their words hit the spot."* That is a disciplined tongue that know how to speak a word in season!

And finally, she wrote, *"A friend is someone who can brighten your day with a simple smile, when others try to do it with a thousand words."* She recognized that when someone is weary the best way to speak to them is with a smile - - a simple gesture of acceptance.

MARK

Mark Farrington's family had moved to Littleton, Colorado when Mark was in the 8th grade. He was the only black student in his class at Ken Caryl Junior High. He had left all his friends behind, his parents were constantly fighting, and he felt like an outcast at school.

Mark felt like the whole world was against him and he began to express his anger by bullying others. But all that changed when he met Rachel. He told us that Rachel looked past his frown, and his anger and saw someone who was hurting.

He and Rachel became friends before his parents moved back to Pennsylvania.

Around 3 years later he had turned on the television and as he watched the news about Columbine he almost went into shock! There on the screen was Rachel's brother, Craig, talking about the death of his sister.

Mark later made a trip out to Colorado and left a handwritten letter on her grave, under a rock. I happened to be going to put roses on her grave that day and probably missed Mark by a few minutes because I found the letter.

As I read the letter, I was deeply moved by what he had written, and I remember wishing that he had left a phone number or an address so that I could contact him.

I read the letter to Sandy and showed it to my children, and even carried it with me to read at several events I spoke it over the next few months.

Here's what his letter said:

My Dear Friend Rachel,

You may not remember me, but that's okay. For my sanity I pray you do. In case you don't, it's me, Mark. The guy who moved to Pennsylvania. Anyways, I don't know where to start or where to go. You touched my life, Rachel. When you met me I was bitter and angry at a world that I felt was cruel and unfair to me.

But it all changed in 8th grade. I met several people who helped me rise from my state of anger. You were one of them, Rachel. You gave me such a positive outlook on life - - and I never said so much as "thank you."

I am so grateful for meeting you. You inspired me. And for that I can't begin to thank you enough. - - - To me you were always a person who seemed to care about yourself, but always seemed to care more for others.

- - - And right here and now, Rachel, I thank you. You helped to give me life, by simply being my friend, and I love you for it. While it's hard, Rachel, I will go on - - we will go on. You're in my heart, my thoughts, and my prayers. And I want you to know one other thing, Rachel; you're admired, you're respected, you're missed, and you're loved. By myself and all who were blessed to know you.

Sincerely,
Mark Anthony Farrington, Jr.

When I finished reading his letter, I took it home with me and have kept it for all these years. It is now one of my most cherished keepsakes from people who have been impacted by Rachel.

I never dreamed that I would come in contact with Mark Farrington - - but I did.

I spoke at La Salle University in Philadelphia a couple of years after I found Mark's letter, and I mentioned his letter in my speech.

To my astonishment, a young man walked up to me and introduced himself as Mark Farrington! We sat down and visited for quite a while and have been friends ever since.

Chapter 11
THE LEGACY BEGINS

In late May, 1999, Josh McDowell called me and asked if I would meet with a group of around 40 national Christian youth leaders. Josh had a condo up near Silverton, Colorado and we all met there.

There were national youth leaders of major denominations such as Presbyterian, Baptist, Pentecostal, Charismatic, Catholic, Lutheran, Methodist, etc. They represented the young people in their respective denominations, which numbered in the millions.

I shared with them about Rachel's kindness to others and I passed out copies of her Codes of Life, and a number of her diary entries. I had no idea of the massive awareness of Rachel's faith and writings that would come out of that meeting.

I immediately began receiving invitations to speak at large gatherings all over the nation. These were crowds that ranged from 3 or 4 thousand to 20 and 30 thousand people. A few were even larger. They took place in football stadiums, sports arenas, and even open fields.

Everywhere I spoke the national media would show up. You can find many of those interviews on YouTube. Rachel's legacy had begun and would immediately reach millions of people around the world.

Soon there was a demand for my two daughters, Bethanee and Dana, to also go and speak at large youth gatherings.

During this time, a major uproar started concerning gun control. Everyone began to blame the guns for the deaths at Columbine. Ironically, the two shooters, Eric and Dylan, recorded a message on video laughing about the fact that we would start passing more laws on gun control, but they said that, "*it won't stop people like us.*"

Sadly, they were right. In the 25 years following the Columbine shootings many more gun laws have been passed, but it has not deterred the school shooting or mass shootings from happening.

Blame began to shift to the National Rifle Association and especially to Charlton Heston, who was president of the NRA at the time. He was the famous actor who starred in movies such as Ben Hur, Soylent Green, The 10 Commandments, Planet of the Apes, and many more.

Charlton Heston heard me in interviews and called me to tell me how grateful he was that I was not accusing him, or the NRA on Rachel's death. The media had portrayed him, unjustly, as a villain because of his position.

He sent our family a copy of "The Bible Tapes" where his famous voice reads the scriptures. He also sent a signed picture from his role in "Ben Hur."

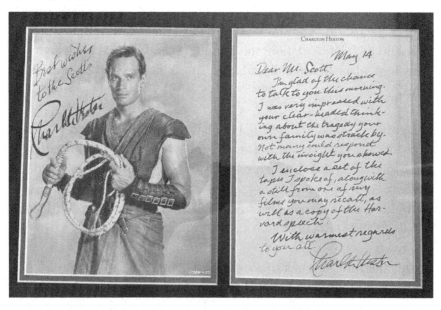

I refused to get drawn into the gun debate because I believed (*and still do*) that it was an issue of the heart.

It was not a gun that decided to kill my daughter, it was a young man who used a gun to do it. Eric and Dylan's weapon of choice were not guns - - it was a bomb made from propane tanks placed in the cafeteria. The guns were only back up instruments to pick of survivors after the blast.

Fortunately, their bomb failed to denotate. If it had, over 500 would have died. I pointed out that if the bomb had gone off, would we be outlawing propane tanks and barbeque grills?

I was shocked by the call from Charlton Heston, because just a couple of days earlier I was talking about him. Two days prior to his call I was sitting at the dining table and felt an urge to write a poem. The words just flowed out as I sat there writing:

> Your laws ignore our deepest needs
> Your words are empty air
> You've stripped away our heritage
> You've outlawed simple prayer
>
> Now gunshots fill our classrooms
> And precious children die
> You seek for answers everywhere
> And ask the question, "Why?"
>
> You regulate restrictive laws
> Through legislative creed
> And yet you fail to understand
> That God is what we need

I read the poem to Sandy and told her that I could almost hear someone like James Earl Jones or Charlton Heston reading it to our nation's leaders. I had no idea that I was about to talk to Charlton Heston, and I certainly never dreamed that I would be speaking to some of our nation's leaders and reading this poem to them!

Less than a week after my phone conversation with Charlton Heston, I received a phone call from a member of Congress asking me to come speak at a House Judiciary meeting at the capitol.

I asked Sandy to go with me, and we flew to Washington D.C. for the meeting. I was ushered back into the "green room" with a bunch of Congressional leaders. When the hearing started, I was ushered in to join a handful of other people who were presenting their opinions concerning gun control.

When my time came, I read from a short speech that I had put together. I also read the poem that I had written just days earlier.

You can see the speech in its entirety on YouTube or watch it through this QR code:

A few minutes after I spoke, Congressman Bob Barr, from Georgia, suggested that they post my poem up beside the 10 Commandments in the Hall of Congress! I was impressed, and felt honored, but I knew that would never happen.

The speech went ballistic on the internet, and I was told that, for a period of time, it was the most read speech on the web.

I learned later that almost every police station in America posted that speech on their bulletin boards.

Many ministers read it from their pulpits on Sunday morning which led to even more invitations to share Rachel's story around the nation.

That speech helped me avoid a major speeding ticket in the state of Florida. I was scheduled to fly in to speak at "Church Without Walls" in Tampa, Florida. My flight took me to Orlando where I was to catch a connecting flight to Tampa.

When I got to the gate in Orlando, they told me that the flight to Tampa had been canceled and I would have to take a rental car or wait for a later flight that night. It was 4:30 p.m. and I was to be speaking at 7:00.

I had no choice but to go to the rental car counter and hope to get to Tampa on time. As it turned out, they only had one rental car available that hadn't been reserved, but there was a lady on my same flight who needed to get to Tampa also.

We agreed to rent the car together and I took the wheel and told the poor lady to hang on. I knew that I had to speed like crazy to get to the meeting on time, so I floored it! Dr. Martin Luther King Jr.'s daughter, Bernice, was the other speaker that night.

I called ahead and told them that I might be running a little late and they agreed to have Bernice go first, giving me a chance to get there. I was going around 100 miles an hour, when suddenly, I was being pursued by a state trooper. My heart sank, because I knew, at that speed, that he would probably take me to the police station.

After I pulled over, he asked me where the fire was, and I told him the situation. He took my license and went back to his vehicle to check me out. After a couple of minutes he came back and said, "*Mr. Scott, we have your speech before Congress posted on our wall and my captain said for me to give you an escort to your destination.*"

The lady riding with me couldn't believe it! We drove at well over the speed limit behind the red and blue lights of the trooper's cruiser into Tampa. I got to the church as Bernice King was finishing her speech!

In the spring of 2000, I was with Josh McDowell and Lou Engel. We started brainstorming around an event that could bring young people from all denominations together for a day of worship in Washington D.C. It was birthed out of Rachel's story and the Columbine tragedy.

Lou Engel took the lead on the project and labeled it, "The Call." It would become one of the largest gatherings in U.S. history with over 400,000 young people attending.

Coach Bill McCartney and I did television interviews to help promote the event. Coach McCartney had just lead the Colorado Buffaloes to a NCAA National Championship.

Craig was with me as I held a flaming torch and challenged that massive crowd of young people to pick up Rachel's torch and make a difference in the world.

Dr. Bill Bright, founder of Campus Crusade *(now known as "Cru")* was one of the speakers. At one point it started raining and Rebecca St. James, a well-known Christian artist who was singing at the event, invited Dr. Bright and I to go to her travel trailer, parked behind the stage, to get out of the rain. I got to spend some quality time with this great man who would pass away 3 years later.

This would be the largest event I would ever speak at. The crowd was larger that the one where a huge number gathered to hear Dr. Martin Luther King, Jr. give his famous "I have a Dream" speech.

At that time, I had so many invitations to share Rachel's story that I began working with a speaking agency to handle all the details of booking, travel, etc. The owner of that agency, Wes Yoder, became a good friend and often traveled with me to events.

I did over 100 college and university campus events during a 2 year period and spoke to huge crowds of students. I spoke at the University of Texas, Auburn, Texas A&M, University of Oklahoma, University of Colorado, Brown University, Princeton, William and Mary College, Colorado State University, University of North Carolina at Chapel Hill, and many, many more.

I remember some of those events more than others. Sandy traveled with me to many of them, and Craig did as well. A number of my close friends also joined me on the road. John Richmond, Wayne Worthy, Matt Hunneywell, Bob Cornuke, Danny Orr, Adam Brandley, Albert Scott, Cory Hollingshead, and Paul Jackson, just to name a few.

I also did 54 events, mostly banquets, for Youth for Christ, where I met some wonderful friends, such as Bob Arnold.

Danny Orr went with me when I spoke at Princeton University. I'll never forget a young Asian student who walked upt to me with tears in his eyes after the event and said, "*Mr. Scott, I walked in here tonight as an atheist, but I am leaving as an agnostic.*" For some reason that go to me and stuck with me all these years.

Danny Orr took a picture of me standing by the statue of Declaration of Independence signer, John Witherspoon. He was a former president of Princeton and this statue stands near the entrance of the place where I spoke.

He is a direct ancestor of Reese Witherspoon.

Danny Orr was drafted by the Oakland A's, but threw his arm out very early in his career. He helped set up a meeting where I spoke with players at the Arizona Diamondbacks headquarters. Danny remains one of my closest friends to this day.

Danny Orr, Darrell, & Diamondback players

Chapter 12
FOSTER AND LYNN FRIESS

Danny Orr had made arrangements for me to speak in the Phoenix Civic Center to a packed crowd. I would meet a man and his wife who would become, not only good friends, but would have an impact on my life for years to come.

Their names were Foster and Lynn Friess. At the end of that meeting a man wearing a baseball cap came up and told me how moved he was by my presentation. He had been sitting at the table with Foster and Lynn, and he looked very familiar.

He told me that he had daughters and that he would be giving them a special hug that night because of Rachel. As he walked away, it dawned on me who he was - - Tom Lehman, the pro golfer who had just been named PGA Player of the Year!

Years later, Tom and his wife, Melissa, joined my son, Mike and I for dinner in Phoenix.

Darrell   Tom Lehman   Mike Scott

After Tom had greeted me at that Phoenix event, Foster and Lynn Friess walked up and introduced themselves. I had no idea that I was meeting two of the most influential people in the world.

Foster had developed the Brandywine Mutual Fund, which became worth over 1 billion dollars. Foster told me that he wanted to help with my infant organization, and he handed me a check. I was used to people handing me a check for $20 or $30 to help out, but as they walked away, I opened it and nearly swallowed my tongue! It was a check for $100,000. I had never seen that much money in my life!

I quickly followed them to thank them and asked Danny Orr to take my picture with Foster and Lynn. Over the next decades they would donate several million dollars to help us reach more and more children across America.

FOSTER FRIESS DARRELL LYNN FRIESS

Foster would become one of my closest friends and we flew to events all over the nation in his private jet. He was one of the most humble, kind, and generous people I would ever come to know.

130

FOSTER ASLEEP ON ONE OF OUR FLIGHTS

I was asked to join the board of a national organization in the year following Rachel's death. I traveled and spoke with that organization and a young attorney by the name of Mike Johnson accompanied me to many of those events. I had no idea that 24 years later, Mike would become Speaker of the House!

Foster had huge influence with politicians on both sides of the aisle and we flew in one of his jets to Washington D.C. in 2017 where he wanted me to speak at the Museum of the Bible. Foster invited a small group of Congressmen and Senators to the event.

The first person to come up to me at that event was Congressman Mike Johnson. He reminded me of our trips together years earlier.

Mike arranged for me to speak at the Shreveport/Bossier Mayor's Prayer Breakfast on November 8, 2018. He joined Sandy and I and a bunch of my cousins for lunch afterward. Mike Johnson told me that his door would always be open to Sandy and I.

Attending the 2017 event at the Museum of the Bible were Senator Tim Scott, Congresswoman Debbie Dingle, Congressman Mike Johnson, Senator Rick Santorum, White House Press Secretary Kayleigh McEnany, and 25 others, including my Uncle Ronald Z. and Aunt Sheila Haymon who I had not seen for years.

Foster Friess had huge influence in Washington D.C. Although he was Republican, he was friends with many Democrats as well. I saw this firsthand in meetings we had with national leaders.

One day while we were in D.C., Foster told his assistant, Steve Munoz, to set up a meeting for Foster and I with Ron DeSantis. DeSantis was running for Governor of Florida at the time and had a busy schedule. But he immediately agreed to meet with Foster and I at his office.

Senator Rick Santorum would become a friend and supporter of Rachel's Challenge, as would Kayleigh McEnany, who would serve on the *Rachel's Challenge* Board of Directors.

Foster Friess   Friends   Darrell   Rick Santorum

Darrell and Kayleigh McEnany

All of these encounters are the result of Rachel's life and legacy. Kayleigh McEnany told Sandy and I that Rachel's story first impacted her in middle school. Rachel became a hero to her all the way through Harvard Law School.

133

Kayleigh dedicated her first book, *The New America Revolution*, to Rachel's memory.

Foster Friess and I played golf all over the country, flew to Mexico for bass fishing, and did many other events together. I miss him.

**My brother, Larry, and I, with Foster
on a bass fishing trip to Mexico**

Foster and Lynn became sweethearts when they were in high school at Rice Lake, Wisconsin. *Rachel's Challenge* did an event at their old school and Foster is seen here putting an imprint of his hand on the "Wall of Challenge," where students for years have taken Rachel's Challenge and left their handprints and names on the wall.

Foster passed away in May of 2021 and we miss him very much. He asked that I speak at his funeral, and I was honored to share time with Rick Santorum, former VP Pence, and others. Many influential people attended his funeral: Laura Ingraham, Tucker Carlson, Dr. Ben Carson, Wyoming Governor Mark Gordan, Charlie Kirk, and others.

Darrell and former VP Pence at Foster's funeral

**Darrell, Sandy, and Rob Unger meeting
with Dr. Ben Carson after Foster's funeral**

Foster was a real Jackson Hole, Wyoming cowboy. He wore his cowboy hat and boots everywhere he went, including meetings with national leaders in D.C. I wrote a poem in Foster's honor and read it at his funeral:

FOSTER'S SHADOW

Out of Rice Lake came a legend who was birthed by destiny
He's a man who loved America and helped to keep it free
He wore leather boots and cowboy hats and loved to tell us jokes
He was friends with global leaders and with all us common folks

He and Lynn became quite wealthy but the used it for the good
Helping victims and the needy in a way that Christians should
Foster gave to many causes and his gifts were never small
He sat tall in the saddle and his shadow touched us all

He would help a struggling waitress through her great financial strain
He would underwrite the victims of a massive hurricane
He supported acts of kindness and compassion in our schools
He gave freely to great ventures while avoiding greedy fools

Both Republican and Democrat would come to love this guy
Who stood firm in his convictions with a twinkle in his eye
Foster had his share of ups and downs, but never did he fall
He sat tall in the saddle and his shadow touched us all

He loved his wife and family, and he loved his friends as well
And all of us had stories that we don't have time to tell
He'll always be remembered in our hearts and minds, but then
Someday we'll pass beyond the veil to greet him once again

"He would do to ride the river with," as all the cowboys say
He walked humbly before his God through each and every day
Foster lived life to the fullest, 'til he heard the Master's call
He sat tall in the saddle and his shadow touched us all

Foster and Lynn would set up a foundation fund for Rachel's Challenge that would be maintained by their grandchildren for decades to come. We are forever grateful to them for their love and generosity. They are a huge part of Rachel's legacy!

Darrell and Sandy meeting with Lynn Friess and her daughter, Traci at the Rachel's Challenge office.

Chapter 13
CHUCK AND GENA NORRIS

The name "Chuck Norris" is known around the globe. Chuck is more than a legend - - he is a mega-legend. He fits in that rare category with Elvis, Houdini, and the Beatles. I used to watch *Walker Texas Ranger* on tv with Rachel and my other kids, without a clue that he and his wife would someday become close friends of ours. Even though that series came out in 1993, there are still millions of viewers who watch reruns every week, around the world.

I first met Chuck and Gena when my son, Craig, and I, were doing an interview on TBN, an international Christian television broadcast. It was the year 2000, and we were all guests on the show. My friend, Paul Jackson, was with us that day and he stood watching with Chuck and Gena while Craig and I were being interviewed. That would begin a lifetime friendship between Sandy and I and the Norris's.

Chuck has a reputation of being a tough guy because of his martial arts skills and his television and movie career, but he is one of the most humble, kind, and thoughtful Christian men that I have ever met. And his wife, Gena, is a superstar in her own right.

Chuck, Gena, and I served on the same board of directors that Mike Johnson served on. Here is a picture of us taken back at that time.

In the years that followed, they would attend my presentations at schools, conferences, and church events. This picture was taken with Sandy and I at a large gathering of multiple churches at a city auditorium in California. It was November of 2003.

While I was speaking at colleges and universities for Campus Crusade (Cru), I took a young man, Matt Hunnewell, with me to Berkeley University in California. We had some spare time on our hands and decided that we would go see a baseball movie that was playing in theaters at that time.

But before we left for the movie, my cell phone rang, and it was Gena Norris. She and Chuck had heard that I was speaking at Berkeley, and at that time they owned a house near there and wanted to know if I could come by and see them. Matt didn't know who I was talking with and I turned to him and asked, "Matt, would you rather go to that baseball movie or go over to Chuck Norris's house to visit?" Of course, he thought I was kidding.

140

Matt was a huge Chuck Norris fan and he nearly had a heart attack when he realized I was telling him the truth. He couldn't believe that I was on the phone with Chuck Norris's wife. We headed over and when we got there, Chuck was doing an interview with Carman, the famous Christian singer.

It was fun to see Matt's excitement as Chuck showed us his home gym and all his trophies. I took this picture of the two of them together that Matt cherishes to this day.

Chuck wasn't just a great martial arts master; he also broke the Great Lakes powerboat record by 26 minutes racing in a speedboat from Chicago into Detroit. He told us about a failed attempt a year earlier with Walter Payton in the boat with him. Chuck was also a great truck racer.

Chuck's son, Eric, won a NASCAR championship and an Emmy Award for his stunt work in Hollywood. My son, Craig, worked on a movie set with Eric Norris.

141

Beth Nimmo (Rachel's mom) and I wrote a book about Rachel titled, *Rachel's Tears*, that became a best seller. On the 10th anniversary of the Columbine tragedy, it was republished. Chuck and Gena wrote the forward for that edition.

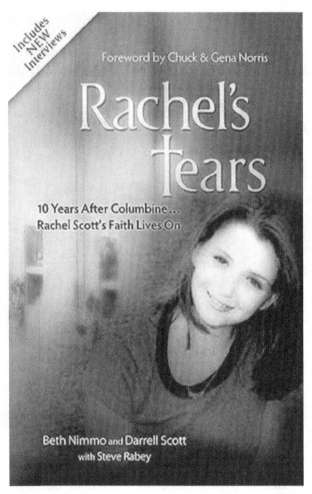

A few years ago, Chuck and I were invited to be guests on the Fox New Channel where he talked about Rachel and the impact that her story was beginning to have on the world. It was the old Hannity and Colmes show. Watch through the QR code at what Chuck had to say:

Chuck wrote his autobiography in a book titled, *Against All Odds*, and dedicated it to Rachel. She would have been thrilled to know that one of her television heroes was impacted enough by her life to dedicate his autobiography to her memory.

If you're a Chuck Norris fan, buy the book. You will discover a lot about him that you didn't know. He was interviewed by Greta Van Susteren on Fox News and talked about dedicating it to Rachel.

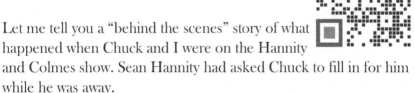

Let me tell you a "behind the scenes" story of what happened when Chuck and I were on the Hannity and Colmes show. Sean Hannity had asked Chuck to fill in for him while he was away.

It was normally Hannity and Colmes entertaining the audience with their back and forth arguments, but this time it would be Norris and Colmes. I got a call from Chuck, and I was delighted when he invited me to be his guest on the show.

Chuck, Gena, and I flew from Houston to New York on a private jet. They also brought a bodyguard along by the name of Darrell. You may be thinking, " *Why would Chuck Norris need a bodyguard?*," but you'll understand in a moment or two.

A limo picked us up and took us to our hotel, and the moment we stepped out of that limo a crowd of people immediately surrounded us. Gena, the other Darrell, and I grabbed hands around Chuck, to prevent the mob from crushing us.

We got into the hotel elevator and another couple rushed up to join us. They didn't recognize Chuck had had just grown a beard and had his cap pulled low on his head.

I knew that they were tourists, and on the way up I asked them where they were from. They replied, *"Germany"* in broken English and then they said, *"We're hoping to meet someone famous while we're here in New York."* None of us said a word!

After they got off the elevator at their floor, we all breathed a sigh of relief. That couple never realized that they were on an elevator with one of the most famous people in the world!

We went into our respective rooms to take a nap and freshen up before the interview. About 3 hours later we headed down to catch the limo and head over to Fox studios.

In the limo, Chuck noticed that Darrell (the other one), the bodyguard, was missing. Gena turned to me and said, *"Darrell would you pretend to be our bodyguard when we get to the studio?"* I said, *"Gena, are you kidding! I would love to be Chuck's bodyguard - - I can't wait to tell my grandkids about this!"*

We all laughed, but once we arrived, once more, I realized why they needed someone to help them keep the mob away from Chuck.

Chuck Norris and Darrell with Alan Colmes on Fox

When we got to the green room, Geraldo Rivera came over and asked us to come to his office. He showed us an old interview from many years earlier where he challenged Chuck to a friendly bout. Geraldo had done some boxing and must have been feeling pretty confident. Needless to say, within seconds, Chuck had him pinned to the floor.

We went back to the green room and Chuck asked me what I thought about some of the notes he had prepared to debate Colmes. I said, *"Chuck, I don't think the audience cares that much about what you say, just give a roundabout kick to Colmes and you'll have their attention!"*

About that time Colmes came into the room to greet us. He was very kind and gracious. Although I differ with a lot of his viewpoints, I found him to be a man of honor. He passed away a few years later.

But I will always cherish the day I got to be Chuck Norris's "bodyguard"!

Chuck and Gena served on our Board of Directors for *Rachel's Challenge* and we awarded them the "Person of the Year Award" at a school that I was speaking at.

The Norris's started a nonprofit organization to teach kids martial arts in Texas schools. It is called *Kickstart Kids.* They teach character development, honor, responsibility, and respect and their program has transformed the lives of many young people.

We created a partnership between *Rachel's Challenge* and *Kickstart Kids*, with *Rachel's Challenge* providing the character development component for their program.

Rachel's Challenge hosted Summit Events for several years where hundreds of teachers, principals, and school superintendents would come for 3 days of inspiration and training. We brought in the best speakers in education for those events. Dr. Robert Marzano, who would become one of my best friends, Dr's. Jim and Charles Fay of *Love and Logic*, Erin Gruwell of *Freedom Writer's*, Christian Moore of *Why Try*, and many others.

One of the highlights of our Summits was when the *Kickstart Kids* would perform their martial arts training for the crowd. Chuck and Gena visited a number of those events with us at our Summits.

In the picture, you can see Chuck and Gena Norris, Sandy and I, and 3 of my children: Craig, Mike, and Dana. In the back right is Rob Unger, CEO of Rachel's Challenge at that time. Behind me to the left is my cousin, Dan Scott, and beside me is my lifetime mentor, Bob Mumford. A very special man is standing beside Chuck in the picture. His name is Cor Suijk, a holocaust survivor and former Director of the Anne Frank House in Amsterdam. I'll write more about Cor later.

At that particular *Rachel's Challenge* Summit, we partnered with the Dallas Holocaust Museum and featured several Holocaust survivors who told their stories and death and torture in the concentration camps during World War 2.

It was the most memorable Summits we ever hosted, and I was glad that Chuck and Gena got to experience it. Our organizations continue to work together, and Sandy and I will forever be grateful for our friendship with these two wonderful people that we love and respect.

Sandy & Darrell Scott   Chuck & Gena Norris Tess & Mark Hanby

Chapter 14
THE ANNE FRANK CONNECTION

As I mentioned earlier, Rachel had read Anne Frank's diary and it inspired her to keep her own diaries. Both girls would die at a young age; both died from the influence of Adolf Hitler; and both would have an impact on millions of people through their diaries.

Did I just say that both would die from the influence of Adolf Hitler? Yes, I did! Everyone knows that Anne died in a concentration camp because of the cruelty of Adolf Hitler to the Jews.

But what most people don't know is that Rachel died on Hitler's birthday - - April 20. That was the date chosen by the two shooters at Columbine because of their obsession with Hitler and the Third Reich. The influence of both good and evil can reach generations of people for decades, and even centuries after their origination.

ANNE FRANK

RACHEL SCOTT

See the QR code to hear about Hitler's influence that took the life of both Anne Frank and Rachel. Two innocent girls would impact the world through diaries.

Eric Harris had a need to control, and a terrible temper, combined with an attraction to violence. His journal was full of violent entries.

He once wrote: *"I want to tear a throat out with my own teeth like a pop can. I want to grab some weak little freshman and just tear them apart like a f*****g wolf. Strangle them, squish their head, rip off their jaw, break their arms in half, show them who is God."*

Eric and Dylan were often seen greeting each other with a "Heil Hitler" salute. They made extremely violent videos in which they rage about what they want to do to students at Columbine.

Both Rachel and Eric Harris, her killer, talked about starting a chain reaction. Rachel wrote in her Codes of Life that she wanted to start a chain reaction of kindness and compassion. Eric wanted to start a chain reaction of death and destruction.

In 2007, Sandy and I went to a local theater to watch a newly released movie called, *"Freedom Writers."* It was about a teacher, Erin Gruwell, who took on an English class filled with gangbangers and violent students. Hillary Swank starred in the movie as Erin.

Erin had a real desire to understand her students and she did amazing things to help them succeed. She got a second job so that she could buy all of them books to read, including the story of Anne Frank. The students got so engrossed in Anne Frank's diary that Erin went out and bought them all diaries. She challenged them to write down their thoughts feelings, etc., and the *"Freedom Writers"* was birthed! Their writings would impact many people through the movie.

Because of the impact Anne Frank had on Rachel's life, I was intrigued in the movie where Erin invited Miep Gies to fly from Amsterdam to meet with her students in California. Miep was the heroic lady who worked for Anne's dad, Otto.

150

She hid and feed the Frank family in the attic before the Nazis finally discovered their hiding place and captured them.

Sandy and I thought that Miep Gies was dead, and we both looked at each other while the movie was playing and simultaneously said, *"She's still alive!"* That was 2007, and Miep would be close to 100 years old! I told Sandy, *"Somehow, we have got to meet her before she dies."*

Later that year I was invited to speak in Rockwall, Texas along with two other national speakers - - and guess what? One of them was Erin Gruwell! I was so excited to meet with her. I was the first speaker on the agenda, and when I finished with Rachel's story, Erin and Maria, one of her former students, came up with tears in their eyes and asked if we could meet after Erin spoke.

Maria Reyes   Darrell   Erin Gruwell

After Erin finished speaking, the three of us got together and talked for at least two hours. During that conversation, I mentioned to Erin that Sandy and I would love to meet with Miep Giess, and Erin said that she would make that happen.

Erin became a close friend to Sandy and I, and over the years she would participate in our *Rachel's Challenge* Summits.

This picture was taken at the Gaylord convention center in Dallas at one of our *Rachel's Challenge* Summits.

Erin had Sandy and I come and speak to all the original Freedom Writers in California.

Erin & our friends, Dr. Robert Marzano & Dr. Jana Marzano at the Rachel's Challenge office

152

Erin introduced us to a man by the name of Cor Suijk, who was a very close friend of Miep Gies. In fact, Cor lived about 100 miles away from Miep's modest condo and would drive over every weekend to make sure that she was okay. He helped her write letters to students and was her caretaker in her final years.

Cor was 19 years old when the Holocaust happened, and although he was not Jewish, he started hiding some of his Jewish friends from the Nazis. He successfully hid 13 families before being caught and captured while hiding the 14th.

He was put into a concentration camp and badly beaten as they tried to get him to tell them where he had hid his Jewish friends. He refused to tell them and as a result he experienced terrible torture and beatings. He lost the use of his left lung from the suffering he endured at the hands of the Nazis.

When World War 2 ended, Cor was released, and his Jewish friends that he had saved were able to come out of hiding. One of those friends introduced Cor to Otto Frank, Anne Frank's dad. Otto was the only one of the Frank family to survive the concentration camps. He lost his wife and two daughters, Anne and Margot.

Cor and Otto became best friends, and, in fact, Cor helped start the Anne Frank House and became its first Director for 10 years.

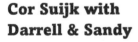

Cor Suijk with Darrell & Sandy

153

Erin Gruwell introduced us to Cor, and he very quickly became a part of the Rachel's Challenge family. He was the oldest speaker that ever represented *Rachel's Challenge*. He was 84 years old when we met him, but for the next few years, until his death, he traveled across Europe sharing both Anne Frank and Rachel's stories with students.

We had Cor to speak at several of our Summits and he always had an impact on the crowds as he shared stories of Otto and Anne Frank.

Debbie Phelps   Cor Suijk

In the picture above you see Sandy and I with two of our friends, who both spoke often at our *Rachel's Challenge* Summits. Debbie Phelps is the mother of Michael Phelps, who we all know has won more Olympic gold medals than any other athlete in history.

Both Debbie and Cor stayed in our home, and we were blessed to hear so many stories that most people never get to hear.

Cor called me in June 2009 and asked if Sandy and I could fly over to Amsterdam and meet with Miep Gies. We were ecstatic at the invitation and immediately booked a flight to go there.

Of all the people Sandy and I have been privileged to meet over the years - - Presidents, entertainers, church leaders, politicians, musicians, etc., Miep Gies is at the head of the list. This brave woman put her own life on the line to save Anne Frank and her family. Cor Suijk would also top that list.

Sandy and I spent a full day with Miep in her modest 4 room condo.

As we sat talking with her, she reached out and took my hand and said, *"Darrell, I am so sorry for the loss of your beautiful Rachel. I never had a daughter, but I understand loss. Anne was like a daughter to me. Not a day goes by that I don't think about her."* I will never forget those words uttered by this dear lady who will always be a hero to Sandy and I!

Miep pointed to scarf hanging on the chair beside me and said, *"That is the scarf that Anne was wearing the day that they came and took them away."*

Then she turned and pointed to an old desk that was behind me and said, *"That was the desk that Anne began writing her diary on before they were captured. Otto gave it to me after he was released from the concentration camp."* I got up and went over to that old desk, and I can't describe the overwhelming feelings I had as I ran my fingers across the very spot where Anne had written the first part of her diary.

Miep could have sold that scarf and desk for millions of dollars, but they were priceless reminders to her of a family, long gone, who she had tried to save.

As we were walking out to the car, with Cor, I turned and saw Miep standing in the doorway waving at us. I quickly snapped a picture, which would turn out to be the last picture ever taken of Miep. She would die a short time later.

The day that we visited with her was June 25, 2009. It was the day that Michael Jackson died. The media would cover his life story and death for weeks. Every time you would turn on the tv it would be another tribute to Michael Jackson.

When Miep died, it barely was mentioned in the news. How screwed up are our ideas about true heroes? Michael was a great entertainer, but his character was in question concerning moral actions toward minors. Miep was a true hero who was willing to die to protect others. Cor Suijk was also that kind of hero.

Miep and Cor were very much involved with the movies made on Anne Frank's life, and Miep won an Oscar for the documentary, *"Anne Frank Remembed."*

At the Summit where you saw Cor and Chuck Norris's picture earlier, I had our videographer, my close friend Bryan Boorujy, film Cor telling the story about the day he met with Adolph Hitler's personal secretary.

It is an amazing story that can be seen with the QR code:

I will forever be grateful to Erin Gruwell for introducing us to Cor Suijk and opening the door for us to meet with Miep Giess.

Anne Frank's influence on Rachel caused my daughter to keep the six diaries that mean so much to our family, and now have been shared with the world.

RACHEL SCOTT'S DIARY

Chapter 15
RACHEL'S FAITH

We are not free to share the whole story of Rachel's life and writings in public schools because of the faith element in her story. We wrote this book to allow the reader access to the full story of her life.

From an early age Rachel seemed to be in tune with the spiritual component of her life. She always showed a propensity toward kindness, compassion, and love for nature, animals, and people.

You can see her conviction for the need of the "Lifemaker" in her life in the diary entry below:

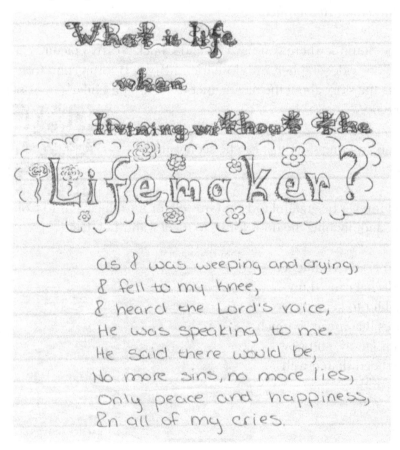

What is life

when

living without the

Lifemaker?

As I was weeping and crying,
I fell to my knee,
I heard the Lord's voice,
He was speaking to me.
He said there would be,
No more sins, no more lies,
Only peace and happiness,
In all of my cries.

For Rachel, her faith was not doctrinal, systematic, nor ritual - - it was personal. She often talked about "an encounter with God" that she had while she was visiting her cousins in Shreveport, LA. She was 11 years old at the time and at the end of a church service she was praying, when she had what she called a "life-changing" experience.

After that experience, our family noticed a change in Rachel. She had always been kind and compassionate, but there seemed to be a deeper dimension of love flowing out of her toward others. For the next 6 years, until her death, she poured herself into helping and serving others. You can see it in her Codes of Life, where she wrote:

"Compassion is the greatest form of love humans have to offer. - - My definition of compassion is forgiving, loving, helping, leading, and showing mercy for others."

Rachel never tried to convert people to her viewpoint by words and arguments. But she did bring about change in people's lives with her love, compassion, and unconditional acceptance of them.

In a book she was writing when she died, titled *"What do I do about God?"*, she wrote:

Before I go off on what you should and should not do . . . I'll start with what I did. I grew up knowing that God exists. A lot of people think that this is enough. IT'S NOT. Acknowledging him is not having a relationship with him.

—Rachel Scott

From a chapter titled, "What do I do about God?" for a book Rachel was in the process of writing

159

There are many people who believe in God that have never had a spiritual awakening. James 2:19 says, *"You believe that there is one God. Good! Even the demons believe that."* According to that scripture, believing in God elevates you no higher than the demon level! *(I sure hope you have a sense of humor as you read my writing)*

Rachel's love for God and others did not come from a place in her head. It came from her heart. It is one thing to know about God with your head, but another thing altogether to know God from your heart.

Her compassion for others caused her to want to serve them. In an ancient writing called the Tao Te Ching, an old Chinese philosopher wrote: "Why is the sea king of a hundred streams?" He answered his own question by saying, "Because it lies below them."

Jesus, 600 years later said it this way: *"Whoever is greatest among you shall be your servant. Whoever exalts themselves shall be abased, but whoever humbled themselves shall be exalted."*

Today the world seems to glorify arrogance, attitude, and pride. Rachel saw the fickleness of outward performance and chose the path of humility and service to others. She wrote:

Break me of my pride, Oh God,

Tear down my string of sins,

This life of filth and worthlessness,

Unto You I willingly give.

Take it from me, all of it,

Do with it what You will.

Take me and mold me God,

Your foundation, begin to build.

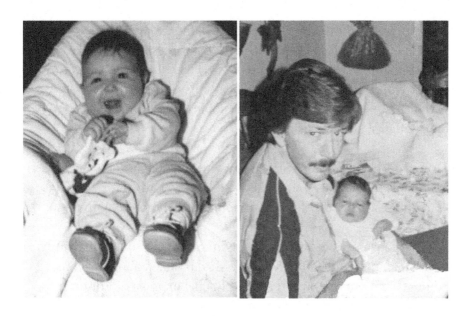

BABY RACHEL   **DAD AND RACHEL**

One of the most spiritual things that Rachel wrote can be found
below. Unfortunately, her words will just sound like gibberish to some
people who have not experienced what she is describing. She was in
tune with the spiritual part of her being, not just the mental part.

Realizations come to me on
            a daily basis
They make everything come
            out of the haze
When they hit me and my
            eyes open and see
It also comes in the form
            of nothing

Many people believe that we are just two-dimensional creatures: body and soul. The Biblical Greek word for body is "soma". The Greek word for soul is "psuche" *(later psyche)*. From the word "psyche" we get the words psychology and psychiatry. Psychologists and psychiatrists are "soul" doctors. The soul is commonly believed to be our thoughts, emotions, and will.

However, there is a dimension that goes even deeper than the soul, and that is the human spirit. The Biblical Greek word for "spirit" is "pneuma". This is a realm of intuition, creativity, and communion.

Many creative people have given credit to a higher source than just the human mind for their creativity. Mozart talked about his music coming from out of nowhere, just as Rachel expressed. Edison credited many of his inventions to dreams.

While cognitive thinking *(from the soul)* contributes much to our lives, metacognitive connection *(from the spirit)* is the source of all true creativity, connectedness, and communion.

Rachel was obviously in tune with God's spirit through her own. That's why she wrote (paraphrase), *"Realizations come to me on a daily basis - - from out of the haze - - and cause my eyes to open!"*

The wisest man who ever live, Solomon, wrote: *"The spirit of man* (and woman) *is the candle of the Lord."* He did not say that the soul was the candle - - but the spirit.

There is a big difference between religion and spirituality. Organized religion has done much to help others, but at times it has done much to harm, as well. Many hungry and poor people have been helped by religious organizations, but many have been hurt and even killed by them. When Rachel wrote about having a relationship with God, she was talking about much more than "going to church", or a synagogue, or a mosque.

True spirituality requires a connection between you and God. A relationship that goes beyond head knowledge. It was Rachel's relationship with God that motivated her compassion for others.

Go after God. Whatever it takes, do it. And don't give the excuse, "I am just a teenager" or "I'll do that when I grow up," because it doesn't work that way. God wants to know you NOW.

—Rachel Scott

From a chapter titled, "What do I do about God?"
for a book Rachel was in the process of writing

I am so glad that Rachel didn't wait until she "grew up" to make that divine connection. You can see her passionate fervor in her writing below:

Those last words, *"I am a warrior for Christ"* was also written on the bottom of her backpack. It reads, *"Living my life as a warrior for Christ."*

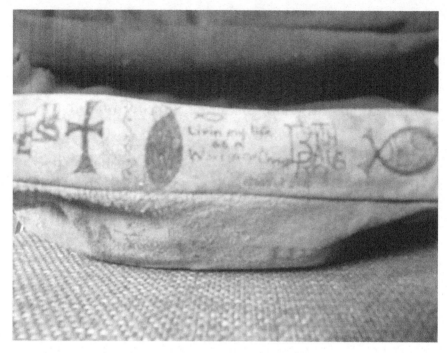

Of course, by being a warrior, she did not mean that she would use a knife or gun, or physical weapon. Her weapons were kindness, compassion, forgiveness, and love. She left all of us the challenge below:

God can't do anything in your life unless you meet him halfway. You have to make room for him. A lot of room.

—Rachel Joy Scott

From a chapter titled "What do I do about God?" from a book Rachel was in the process of writing

Chapter 16
BERMUDA, SOUTH KOREA, JAPAN, MEXICO, AUSTRALIA, TASMANIA, IRELAND, AND BEYOND

Rachel's story has been told in live events around the world to over 35,000,000 people.

Over a period of 3 years, several speakers from our *Rachel's Challenge* team were in Bermuda speaking in every school on the islands there. Sandy and I went several times to participate. Our sponsor was a large church there, where I spoke several times.

They started Friends of Rachel Clubs in most of those schools and it had a huge impact on the entire country of Bermuda. The television stations covered many of our events there.

The most prominent television program in South Korea did a nationwide broadcast that featured Rachel's story. A news crew from Japan came to our *Rachel's Challenge* office and produced an hour long show featuring Rachel's life and legacy.

Sarah Blakely, a young lady from Ireland was so intrigued by Rachel that she raised money to bring Sandy and I to her beautiful country to share Rachel's story with many young people there.

In late August 2006, Hillsong Church in Sydney, Australia had me to come and speak at several events. My brother, Larry, went with me. I will never forget a comical moment that occurred with my brother, Phil Dooley, who was our host, and myself.

We were having lunch in a café just across the bay from the world famous Opera House in Sydney, when I noticed Larry was really focused on gazing across the bay. While Phil and I were engaged in conversation about the upcoming event in the Olympic Center - - suddenly my brother interrupted our conversation.

165

Larry has always called me "Bubba", since I'm his older brother. He blurted out, *"Bubba, I've seen that building somewhere before!"* Phil had just taken a big swig of his beverage and he spewed it out all over the table, exclaiming, *"You've got to be kidding me mate!"*

Larry was pointing at the Opera House - - one of the finalists for the 7 Wonders of the modern world! It is one of the most recognizable buildings on planet earth! I have never let him live that one down, and we still laugh about it today.

Later that day Phil Dooley was driving us back to our hotel when we came to a red light and stopped. It was a dead end, requiring us to either turn right or left. Straight ahead was a church building just past the red light. Suddenly a car came flying by on the right side of our vehicle and ran the red light, jumping a small ditch and crashing right through the side of the church building!

This is a picture that appeared in the Sydney newspaper the next day.

Phil pulled his car over and Larry and I rushed inside the church building. The driver was still sitting in the car, dazed, but unharmed. He was paraplegic and his hand operated accelerator malfunctioned.

166

Instead of being able to stop at the red light, his car had accelerated, and he hit the side of the church building full blast. It is amazing that he survived!

The next day preparations were being made for the big event in the Olympic Center there in Sydney. That evening the arena was filled with thousands of young people who came to hear Rachel's story. The Hillsong band and singers started the event and then I spoke for over an hour. It was a powerful event that changed the lives of many people that night.

A couple of days later Larry and I were in Tasmania where I spoke at another large event with over 8,000 attending. Our host took us to the zoo where we got to see Tasmanian Devils. I didn't even know they were real animals, since my only exposure to them was as a young boy watching Bugs Bunny cartoons that included Tasmanian Devils.

While I was in Australia, arrangements were made for me to fly back the following year and meet with Steve Irwin, the famous "Crocodile Hunter." I really looked forward to meeting him, but the day Larry and I fly back to the United States was the day he was killed by a sting ray while filming an episode. It was Sept. 4, 2006.

On the flight back to the states, we had an incident that took place on the airplane. A man who was high on drugs started screaming and punching people. He was quickly subdued by an air marshal who was on the flight, so we had to turn around in the middle of the Pacific ocean and take the man to the island of Fiji to turn him over to authorities there. It caused our flight to last 4 hours longer than usual.

In 2006, our friends, Mark and Tess Hanby invited us to go with them to Guadalajara, Mexico to meet with a very influential family to share Rachel's story. We did not realize, at the time, that this would start a chain reaction of kindness throughout the country of Mexico!

167

The Maldonado family own businesses all across Mexico, and even some in the U.S.A. They have tens of thousands of employees and are very influential throughout their country.

The whole family got behind the concept of bringing Rachel's Challenge to Mexico, especially Joel Maldonado. Joel had me and one of our speakers, Ali, to come back in 2017 to Guadalajara and launch the program.

The following pictures show several events that kicked off the *Rachel's Challenge* program that has now grown to include many schools in multiple cities in Mexico.

KICKOFF EVENT IN TEPIC, MEXICO

ALI SPEAKING AT A SCHOOL

1ER ENCUENTRO, **TEPIC NAYARIT, MÉXICO.** www.rachelschallengemexico.org

ANOTHER SCHOOL EVENT IN TEPIC, MEXICO

JOEL MALDONADO AND DARRELL WATCHING

PART OF THE GUADALAJARA RC STAFF

In 2018 there was a big celebration in Guadalajara with over a thousand students coming together to celebrate a year's worth of acts of kindness, demonstrated through chain links. The Maldonado family flew our family and some of our staff to the event in one of their private jets.

Don & Bethanee, Craig, Darrell & Sandy, Mike

ABOVE: 2018 RACHEL'S CHALLENGE CELEBRATION
BELOW: DARRELL, SANDY, AND MIKE SCOTT

In 2019 I flew back to Mexico with my friend, Mark Hanby, and we met with members of the Maldonado family for lunch, as we have many times since.

MARK & DARRELL WITH MALDONADO'S

Our team in Mexico continues to reach thousands of young people every year. The goal for *Rachel's Challenge* in Mexico is to be in every major city within the next few years.

Bermuda and Mexico have been two of the nations that have embraced us the most.

However, our speakers have been to many countries around the globe such as Canada, China, Latin America, and many more.

Rachel's legacy will continue for many decades after I am gone, and after this book has disappeared from bookshelves.

172

Chapter 17
FRIENDS OF RACHEL CLUBS

We have been told by thousands of principals and superintendents that our school assembly programs are the most powerful that they have ever experienced.

All our videos and presentations are age appropriate. For, example in our elementary assemblies we do not talk about Rachel's death or show any pictures of Columbine. We focus on Rachel's acts of kindness through video re-enactments and photos of her.

Our middle school and high school programs are very emotionally impactful because of our videos and stories that are geared for their age groups.

We saw tremendous change take place in our assemblies, as students began to reach out to one another, as well as to their teachers and parents.

I remember a phone call from a mother of a middle school parent who asked, *"What did you do to my son?"* At first I thought the phone call was going to be negative, but immediately found that it was a very positive one.

She was a single mom with 3 children and her son attended the middle school that one of our speakers had just presented at. She told me that her son had hardly spoken to her in two years. When she would ask him questions, he would just mutter back quick responses. He never helped her around the house.

But she said that all that changed the day *Rachel's Challenge* came to his school. He came home that day and gave her a hug and said, *"I love you mom!"* She was shocked beyond belief! Not only did he tell her he loved her, he started cleaning his room.

But as powerful as our assemblies proved to be, we had quite a few educators ask about what we could do to follow up the assemblies.

After much thought and planning, we decided to train our speakers to create "Friends of Rachel" clubs in the school. Following the assembly, they would take up to 100 students into a smaller room and do a 90 minute training to launch their club.

Eventually we shortened the name, "Friends of Rachel" to FOR clubs. We emphasized that we were for things, not against them. What you put your focus on is what you become. There are well intended programs out there that focus on bullying and the result is that bullying often increases. Our focus is on kindness and compassion, and we see bullying decrease in every school we go into.

So we are for things, not against them. We are not against bullying, we are for kindness. We are not against insulting, we are for complimenting. We are not against anger, we are for compassion. I think you get the drift.

As great as our results were through our assemblies, we were amazed at the amplification of Rachel's legacy through the FOR Clubs.

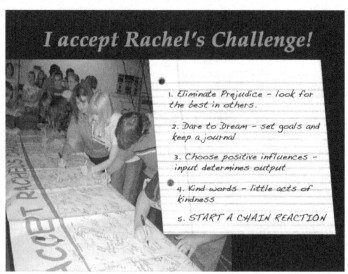

We began to see stories like this one, where students made 1,000 paper cranes for a classmate who was diagnosed with cancer.

4A Saturday, February 28, 2009   The Journal News   WP   Communities

Cranes of hope touch boy with cancer, family

Diana Costello
The Journal News

PLEASANTVILLE — Japanese legend promises that folding 1,000 origami cranes will bring about wishes for a speedy recovery from illness and a long life.

At only 14 years of age, Brendan Klein already needs that legend to hold true.

The Pleasantville Middle School eighth-grader is in the midst of a battle with leukemia, and his classmates started folding 1,000 paper cranes after he was diagnosed in September.

In a special ceremony yesterday morning, students presented the colorful bouquet of assorted patterns to Brendan and his family, along with wishes for a quick return to health.

In turn, the family has passed the 1,000 cranes on to the Maria Fareri Children's Hospital in Valhalla, where Brendan goes for treatment.

"You may think it's a small thing to fold one paper crane," Russell Klein, Brendan's father, told the students after accepting the gift. "But you have no idea how big it is for us and how much it means."

The 1,000 cranes came about as part of a new school club, called Rachel's Challenge. The club's mission is to reach as many people as possible with the message of kindness and compassion. Rachel's Challenge is a national group that started in honor of Rachel Scott, who was the first person killed in the Columbine High School tragedy in Colorado.

The whole project is based on a chain reaction of kindness," said Barbara Brandenburg, a guidance counselor at the middle school.

Saying the gift was "cool," Brendan thanked his friends and expressed relief that his life is slowing getting back to normal. He had to spend a week in the hospital after being diagnosed, and now goes back at least once a week for chemotherapy.

"It's nice to be home and just relaxing, playing on the computer, eating great food and having my friends over," he said

The project for Brendan may

Members of the FOR Club at his school spent hours putting together 1,000 paper cranes to show their support for Brandon.

Watch the news story about the paper cranes:

Students that were members of the FOR Clubs began to come up with great ideas to help their fellow students, their schools, and their entire communities.

FOR Clubs have created what they call a "Rachel's Pantry" where they take an unused classroom and convert it into a food pantry. They stock it full of nonperishable food items donated by local grocery stores and food banks so that no one in their school goes hungry. Many students go to school each morning with no breakfast, because their family can't afford it. Students have free access to everything in the "Rachel's Pantry".

Soon after the start of the pantries, FOR Clubs added "Rachel's Closet", where students could have access to any type of clothing they needed. These items are not "hand me downs", but are fashionable clothes and shoes donated from stores and individuals.

Rachel Closets are now in schools all across the United States where students can get clothing they need with no pressure or embarrassment.

A STUDENT STOCKING RACHEL'S PANTRY

STUDENTS STOCKING RACHEL'S CLOSET

We were so blessed when we realized how many thousands of students all over the nation were willing to volunteer in the pantries and closets to help those in their school who are less fortunate. Rachel's legacy has created millions of acts of kindness that touch, not only the hearts, but the stomachs and bodies of many young people.

177

In the early days of *Rachel's Challenge*, while I was still speaking in schools, I presented at a large high school in California. After the presentation, I went to a smaller room to train around 100 students for the Friends of Rachel (FOR) Club.

There was a large young man who had been deeply impacted by the assembly presentation that seemed hesitant about being in the training. After I started the training session, he raised his hand and asked if he could be dismissed.

Knowing that he had been moved by Rachel's story, I asked him why he wanted to leave. I was stunned at his answer. He said, *"I'm not qualified to be a part of this club, Mr. Scott. I've done some very bad things and I've bullied a lot of people in this room."*

I found out after the training that his name was "Odie", and he was a gang leader in a pretty violent gang in town. I told Odie that I didn't want him to leave, and that he was exactly the kind of person I wanted to help lead the FOR Club. All the other students started clapping and Odie stayed.

ODIE

178

Not only did he stay, but he became the leader of the FOR Club in his high school. He and I had a long heart to heart conversation after the training and as I hugged him and went to leave, he looked at me and made a promise that Rachel's story had changed him forever.

Almost a year after that school event, I received a letter from the school counselor. Included in that letter was a picture of Odie. She wrote that Odie had died in a motorcycle accident on his way to help fight fires that had broken out in California. She said that Odie had turned his life around and had become a great example of kindness to all the students in his school.

Every time I led a FOR training after that, I dedicated it to the memory of Odie.

Some schools have "Hands of Rachel" walls where students can trace an outline of their hands, like this one that I showed earlier in the book.

In Jan. 2009, *Rachel's Challenge* went to Catskill High School in a small town in New York. The most popular student in the school was a young man by the name of Victor. He was captain of the soccer team and president of the student council.

He was deeply moved by Rachel's story and became the leader of the Friends of Rachel Club in his school. Victor signed the banner and he told Dave, the speaker from *Rachel's Challenge*, that he was going accept the challenge and make a difference in his school and community.

Victor knew that the local Shriner's Hospital needed money to help with their children's programs, and so he had an idea. He organized his FOR Club and told them that they were going to fill up the back of their principal's pickup truck with tabs from aluminum cans. They would turn the tabs into cash for a donation to the Shriner's Hospital. Although the idea was a noble one, no one realized how many tabs it would take to fill up the back of a pickup truck.

So, they started collecting tabs, but it was getting close to the end of the school year and they were getting discouraged. They only had enough tabs to fill up about a third of the truck bed.

Then something happened that nobody expected. Victor died in an automobile accident. The whole school was devastated by Victor's death, and they wanted to do something to honor his memory.

Someone got the idea of finishing the project that Victor had started, to fill up the principal's truck with the aluminum tabs. So they contacted the *Rachel's Challenge* office in Colorado and in turn *Rachel's Challenge* contacted all the Friends of Rachel Clubs within a 50 mile radius of Catskill High.

Thousands of tabs poured in over the next few weeks, and the Club was able to reach Victor's goal! As the last car, bringing tabs, pulled away someone took this picture of the pickup truck loaded with tabs.

Then they noticed that the last car had been dripping liquid on the ground, and it spread out in the form of a heart!

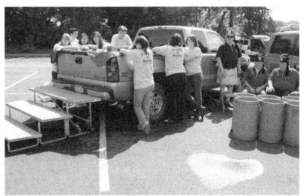

In 2010, the Catskill Friends of Rachel decided to honor Victor's memory by filling up 2 pickup trucks with tabs. Their goal was to collect over 2 million tabs, breaking a world record! And they did!

Victor would be thrilled to know that his dream to help hospitalized children became a reality.

To see the complete story about Victor, see the QR code:

All the schools in Rockwall, Texas got involved with *Rachel's Challenge*. After having our programs in their schools for several years, Family Circle Magazine put out an article in August of 2009 about the top 10 cities for parents to raise their children. Guess which town was listed as number 1? *Rachel's Challenge* was the "Gold Star" reason for Rockwall's success.

ROCKWALL TEXAS

Terry Crabtree, a 50-year-old part-time nurse, has attended every single football game and marching competition since her son, Zach, 17, a sports nut and trombone player, started at Rockwall-Heath High School. Her husband, J.C., 57, who owns a carpet cleaning business, coached Zach's soccer and softball teams at the Y, and Terry has even filled in for the staff nurses at all the schools Zach and his sister, Jessica, 19, have attended. The

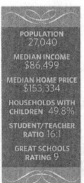

POPULATION
27,040

MEDIAN INCOME
$86,499

MEDIAN HOME PRICE
$153,334

HOUSEHOLDS WITH
CHILDREN 49.8%

STUDENT/TEACHER
RATIO 16:1

GREAT SCHOOLS
RATING 9

Crabtrees aren't unusual but the norm. "There are so many moms and dads stepping up, you practically have to get on a waiting list," says J.C. "We all want to show that we care about what our kids do." This lakeside Dallas suburb is one of the fastest-growing communities in Texas but still possesses the qualities the Crabtrees value most. Area schools rank among the top in the state on standardized test scores. And close ties are formed in the classroom. Jessica's third grade teacher still sends her a birthday card every year, while Zach's middle school music instructor invites him to his jazz-band gigs around town. "The educators are not only top notch," says Terry, "they're terrific human beings as well."

GOLD STAR Rockwall was the first school district in the nation to adopt Rachel's Challenge, a K-12 education program encouraging kids to perform random acts of kindness, named after Rachel Scott, the first student killed at Columbine High.

Under the leadership of school counselor, Nancy Boyd, and Superintendent of Schools, Dr. Gene Burton, Rockwall became the best town in America to raise children. They oversaw the activities of all the FOR Clubs in all the schools in Rockwall.

"Letters of Kindness" is another project that FOR Clubs get involved with. They periodically write letters of kindness to people who touch their lives: bus drivers, cafeteria workers, teachers, parents, police officers, fire fighters, etc.

Principal Virdie Montgomery has become one of my closest friends. As principal of Wylie, Texas High School, he allowed us to film his FOR Club doing activities that are performed all over the nation.

Another one of those projects is the "New Student Program" in which all the FOR Club members reach out at lunch time and throughout the day to new students at school.

The "Student Outreach Program" activates the FOR Clubs into a variety of ways to serve both individuals and communities. Feeding the hungry in homeless programs. Planting trees, cleaning up parks, or painting houses for the elderly. The opportunities for these FOR Clubs is unlimited!

There are so many activities that I could give stories about, but that would fill up a book in itself! Needless to say, Rachel's legacy lives on through the acts of kindness practiced by FOR Clubs.

Watch this powerful video on how the Friends of Rachel Clubs are bringing people together! It has helped create a "family" for schools everywhere.

Chapter 18
CHAIN REACTION PROGRAM

In Rachel's Codes of Life, she wrote about starting a chain reaction of kindness. From the beginning of *Rachel's Challenge*, we have encouraged students to record acts of kindness on pieces of paper and turn those into paper chains that can be hung throughout the school.

Rachel's Challenge had been in thousands of individual schools, but the first entire school district to embrace us from kindergarten through high school was the Rockwall, Texas school district headed up by Dr. Gene Burton, who has become one of my closest friends.

The chain link project would eventually evolve into a full blown "Chain Reaction Day" in schools. But before I get to that part, please watch the entire video on how it all started, beginning with elementary schools.

The chain links became a part of every school from that point on.

CHAIN LINKS FROM ALL ACROSS AMERICA

After watching the movie, *Freedom Writers*, and talking with Erin Gruwell, the teacher that the movie was about, we decided to start an all day program that we call, "*Chain Reaction.*"

We limit the number of student participants to 100 and invite up to 20 adults (teachers and parents) to help administrate the day's activities. It is an intensively interactive program that includes whole group activities, short teaching lessons, small group interactions, and one on one student activities. The results are phenomenal!

One of our activities includes breaking the group down into groups of 5 students and 1 adult. The activity is called, "If you really knew me". Each participant, including the adult, has 2 minutes each to let the others know something about themselves that they seldom share, or have never shared with others.

Sandy and I participated in several of these around the country and we always end up laughing and crying with the students throughout the day.

In one session that I participated in, a young girl who looked a lot like Taylor Swift, opened up to the group that her stepdad and her uncle repeatedly raped her and threatened to kill her and her mom if she ever revealed what was happening. Needless to say, we were all shocked. We wept with her and assured her that we would make sure that she and her mom would be protected and that her stepdad and uncle would never do that again.

At the end of the day all the adults are required to meet with school counselors and report any activities like that one, and the school and police force followed up to ensure that young girl and her mom's protection. While that was an extreme example, we hear horror stories in almost every Chain Reaction Day.

Another activity that occurs at the end of the day is an open mic session, where anyone, adult or student can share their heart with the rest of the group.

One of our speakers reported that at the beginning of the day when everyone sits in a large circle and introduces themselves, there was a local minister who came to "help out the kids". He was decked out in a suit and tie and introduced himself as "Reverend - - - ." The students were all immediately turned off by his self-righteous attitude.

As the day progressed, he began to loosen up and eventually took off his tie. Then off came his suit coat. Then he rolled up his sleeves. By the end of the day, he was joking, crying, laughing, and having fun with the students.

When it came time for the open mic session, he was one of the first ones to go up front. A hush grew over the crowd as he began to weep and share with the group that when he was a young boy, he had been sexually abused by a youth pastor. He had reported it to his parents and the main pastor, but no one did anything about it.

He told them that he had never told anyone about that incident, not even his wife. He said, *"I want to apologize to any of you that have ever been mistreated in any way by a pastor, a youth pastor, or any other religious leader in your life."*

The students all formed a circle around him, crying with him and showing their love and comfort for him. Our speaker told us that it was a moment that he will never forget!

Another activity that we do on Chain Reaction Day is called, "Cross the Line." We have both a male and female instructor that participates with the students all day and they take turns asking questions to the entire group. Everyone is placed on one side of the gym or large room that we are in.

187

As the questions are asked, students are asked to cross the line if the answer for them personally is "yes." The questions begin with easy answers, such as, "if you like wearing jeans to school, cross the line."

But they slowly get more and more serious and personal. "If you have ever been bullied because of your size, cross the line." "If you have every bullied another student, cross the line." "If you have ever had thoughts of taking your own life, cross the line."

The students who don't cross the line are asked to be respectful of those who do and if they feel empathy for those crossing the line, they can put their hand over their heart.

You would have to experience that activity to see how powerful it is! At the end of the day, those who have bullied other students are openly apologizing and giving the ones they have bullied hugs.

One of the most powerful examples came from a young man who was known to be a bully in his school. He was deeply moved by Rachel's story and told the speaker that he wanted to do something to let the whole school know how sorry he was for the way he had treated them.

Our speaker told him to go somewhere quiet, and get still and the answer would come to him. At the end of the school day, that young man stood outside the school entrance with a sign held high over his head that simply said, "I'm sorry!" Click on the QR code below to watch a powerful video of what happened.

You could never have forced or bribed that young man to stand out there and hold that sign over his head as he walked back and forth in front of the buses. But Rachel's story - - her life - - and her writings, did what nothing else could do. It brought instant change to his life!

The video accessible through the QR code below shows just how powerful a Chain Reaction Day can be.

If you want to see a full comprehensive documentary about the 3 part series that was produced by Channel 7 in Denver, Colorado, through the QR codes below.

 RACHEL'S STORY PART 1

RACHEL'S STORY PART 2

 RACHEL'S STORY PART 3

189

Chapter 19
WAR ON THE SHORE

The feud had been going on for 50 years. It was comparable to the infamous Hatfield and McCoy's story. Except this was not just a feud between 2 families. It was a bitter feud between 2 Michigan towns and the battle centered around their annual football game, which they called, *"The War on the Shore."*

Oscoda, Michigan is a small town of about 1,000 people located on the east shore of Lake Huron. It is 87% white with the rest being native American and Asian. No black citizens live there.

10 miles south of Oscoda is Tawas, Michigan, also located on the east shore of Lake Huron. It has around 1,800 residents with 97% white residents and approximately 40 black residents.

The rivalry between the two towns started a half century ago between the town's football teams, but it quickly spread to the whole population of both towns.

There are 22 churches and 33 counseling centers between the two towns that have dozens of fulltime pastors, priests, rabbis, psychologists, psychiatrists, and counselors available - - but none of them could bring a truce - - much less peace, to the two communities.

The hatred and bitterness began to escalate over the years until students were starting to commit felonies. There were fights breaking out. Students from one school were spray painting the buses of their opponent school, placing toothpicks on the practice fields so that players would be injured, defecating on the school grounds, and more.

It got so bad that the Michigan state police were called in to investigate some of the activity.

It was during that time that I spoke at an educational conference in Michigan, and state trooper, Jennifer Pintar, happened to be one of the attendees. She was so moved by the presentation that she went back and told her senior officer that they needed to provide the funds for bringing *Rachel's Challenge* into both schools.

Trooper Jennifer Pintar
Michigan State Police

They contracted with us to send a speaker to both high schools, but failed to tell us about the hostile environment, or that both schools were almost totally white students.

We sent one of our young speakers who had just gone through training to do the job. It was only her 3rd time to present *Rachel's Challenge*. Her name is Keyona.

KEYONA

191

I'll never forget the day Keyona called our office from Oscoda and in a trembling voice she told us that she was scared. She said that she was the only black person that she had seen in either town, and then she added, emphatically, *"These people hate each other!"*

We tried to calm her down by assuring her that the opening video would give her the leverage she needed to challenge the schools to acts of kindness, but to be honest, our confidence was a little shaken as well.

The two school assemblies took place on the week of the annual *"War on the Shore"* football game between the two towns, so everyone in both locations were already fired up by their hatred for their opponents.

But a miracle was about to happen! After Keyona finished with the assembly in Oscoda, the students in the FOR Club training suggested that at the football game, Friday night, the two groups of opposing fans should join hands on the field at half-time as a show of reconciliation and unity.

OSCODA FOOTBALL PLAYERS

192

Amazingly all the students agreed to get on board with the idea. It was the adults that were doubtful about it.

Keyona went to Tawas the next day and introduced the idea at their FOR Club training session, and the students there agreed to get on board with the idea.

TAWAS FOOTBALL PLAYERS

You must watch the video through the QR code to get the full impact of this story. I promise you that it will inspire you!

Friday night rolled around, and the game started. At half-time, the announcer asked for anyone who wanted to show a sign of reconciliation to go down on the field and join hands.

At first there was a moment of hesitancy, but then students from both sides began to pour out on the field, followed by the adults.

When the Oscoda football team came out of the locker room the players ran to the other side of the field to join hands with their opponents. People were in tears as they saw a miracle unfolding before their very eyes.

193

Needless to say, a young black lady brought peace to 2 all white towns that had been at each other's throats for decades! She told Rachel's story and accomplished something in 3 days that 55 churches and counseling centers were not able to do in 50 years!

I do not mean to imply that the churches and counseling centers were ineffective. I'm sure that they helped a lot of people in those towns over the 50-year period. But they couldn't get rid of the hatred between the 2 towns like *Rachel's Challenge* did.

I can almost visualize the imaginary headlines the day following the game:

DAILY NEWS

World - Business - Finance - Lifestyle - Travel - Sport - Weather

Issue: 240104   THE WORLDS BEST SELLING NATIONAL NEWSPAPER   Est - 1965

First Edition   Monday 5th June

FEUD ENDS AFTER 50 YEARS!

Inexperienced young black lady brings peace and harmony to a fifty year feud between two all white towns in three days by telling a story!

Young Keyona Williams, speaker for Rachel's Challenge, with very little speaking experience spoke at two towns that have been feuding for over fifty years. After sharing an amazing story about the first victim at Columbine High School back in April of 1999, the students and staff had an incredible transformation which reconciled the two towns after fifty years of feuding.

Rachel's Challenge doesn't just touch individuals. It has an impact on school districts like Rockwall, Texas, towns like Oscoda and Tawas, cities like San Diego and Atlanta, and even entire nations like Bermuda and Mexico. The drawing of her hands and her statement *"These hands belong to Rachel Joy Scott and will someday touch millions of hearts"* has become a reality!

Chapter 20
PAUL'S ANCHORS, NOAH'S ARK, & RACHEL'S VALLEY

MALTA

Bob Cornuke is a friend of mine. He also happens to be the "real" Indiana Jones. He is a former S.W.A.T team detective and had traveled extensively with former astronaut Jim Irwin, a man who had walked on the moon.

Bob has made amazing discoveries and participated in incredible adventures in search for Biblical artifacts and locations. He has been involved in revealing the potential locations of the Ark of the Covenant in Ethiopia, the anchors from Paul's shipwreck, the location of Noah's ark, the real Mt. Sinai, and the location of the final Jewish temple (which is not the "Temple Mount").

I spoke together with Bob Cornuke, Josh McDowell, and David Barton in some of the largest churches in America for over a year working with Brannon Howse in Worldview Conferences.

During this time, Bob and I became close friends and found out that we lived only 20 minutes apart near the Denver, Colorado area. We golfed together with our wives, vacationed together in Bermuda and Bob traveled with me to quite a number of events that I was speaking at.

Darrell with Bob Cornuke

Bob is one of the best, engaging speakers I have ever heard. In early May of 2002, he asked me if I would like to be part of an adventure in Malta. He had done a lot of research on Paul's shipwreck from Acts 27 and was fairly convinced that the location used by tourists today, St. Paul's Bay, was not the real location.

Acts 27 gives a lot of detail concerning the location where the shipwreck occurred.

It had to be a part of the coastline of Malta that the seasoned sailors did not recognize. It had to be a place where two seas met in stormy weather. It had to be a bay with a visible beach. There had to be a reef where the ship would be torn apart. There had to be 90 feet of depth where they dropped 4 massive anchors. The anchors had to be from a 1st century Roman grain ship. (for more details on this story go to www.baseinstitute.org)

Bob's research concluded that only one location fit the description around the coastline of Malta, on the south end of the island in the Mediterranean Sea. He believed that the anchor stocks, made of around 400 pounds of lead, would still be in existence. The wood part of the anchors would have long ago been dissolved.

Bob made trips to Malta, before I went, and discovered that divers had found four 1st century anchors in 90 feet of water, at a place where two seas meet, by Muxnar reef in a bay that would not have been recognized by 1st century sailors: St. Thomas Bay! The year was 1971 when they found them.

The traditional location, named by the Catholic Church, is on the north side of Malta and not only does it not come close to fitting the Biblical location, but no 1st century Alexandrian freight ship anchors have ever been found there.

There is no reef, no place where two seas meet, etc.

This is what a 1st century Alexandrian or Roman grain ship anchor would have looked like. The stock is the lead piece that runs across the top, with a hole in the middle where the wood shaft was placed.

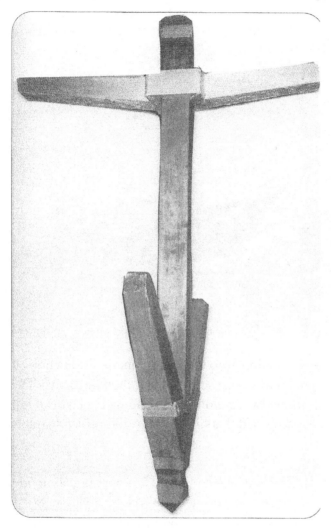

In his previous trips to Malta, Bob was able to track down the first 3 anchors but the fourth was unaccounted for. My close friend, Bryan Boorujy, who would later become the videographer for *Rachel's Challenge*, was also going with us to film re-enactments of the anchors being raised out of the sea.

After a few days of filming in St. Thomas Bay, Bob brought all the divers together who had found the first 3 anchor ballasts for dinner at a historic restaurant, The Black Pearl, an old ship that had once been owned by Errol Flynn and had been converted into a restaurant. It was the main prop in the movie, Popeye, starring Robin Williams.

Charles Grech, a diver who had found one of the anchors, told Bob that he might know where he could find the fourth one. The fourth anchor was found by a famous diver who had been dead for several years. But Charles said that his widow would probably still have the anchor.

He knew which village she had once lived in, but had no idea what her address was, or if she even still lived in that village. So, the three of us got in his car the next day and headed to a medium sized village on the south part of Malta.

When we got there, I was looking at the multitude of homes and small businesses and thinking, *"There is no way we are going to find this lady's house, even if she still lives here."*

198

We parked in front of an old church that had been battered by bombing from World War II and still had a few scars to prove it. We got out of the car and a man happened to be walking by and Charles spoke to him in Italian and asked if he knew where the widow of this certain diver was. (*I don't remember the diver's name*)

To our amazement, the man pointed to a house two doors down from where we were standing! We went over to the big wooden door and Charles knocked, and asked Bob and I to step back. The lady cracked open the door and peered out and she and Charles began to talk. Bob and I could not understand what they were saying, but evidently, Charles was convincing, because she invited us in.

We sat down in her living room and Charles began to translate questions from Bob.

"Do you know if your husband ever talked about finding a large Roman or Alexandrian anchor from St. Thomas Bay?" She looked at us tentatively before nodding her head *"yes"*.

"Do you know what he did with the anchor?" Again, a slow nod, *"yes"*. *"Do you know where the anchor is now?"* A repeated nod. *"Can you tell us where it is?"* This time there was a long pause, and then she stood up and beckoned for us to follow her. Her house was the typical Italian U-shaped home with an open courtyard.

She took us to her outdoor courtyard where flowers and plants were growing - - and what happened next is another one of those unbelievable moments.

There was a slight mist falling and it was cloudy overhead, but just as we walked out into her courtyard, a ray of sunshine broke through the clouds and lit up the fourth anchor that was on a ledge in her small garden! Bob and I looked at each other and I expected to hear angels start singing, *"Hallelujah!"*

Well - - that didn't happen, but it was one of those moments in time that I will never forget. Here we were in the 21st century, looking at a 1st century Roman/Alexandrian anchor stock that was very likely from Paul's shipwreck.

Bob Cornuke and I with the anchor found by Charles

Can we prove that it was from Paul's shipwreck? Yes we can! We found a handwritten note, verified by Sotheby's Auction, taped to that anchor in Paul's handwriting saying, *"Bob, Darrell, and Charles. I'm so glad you found this fourth anchor. I am validating it for you. Sincerely, the Apostle Paul."*

No! Of course we can't say 100% that it was - - but if I were a betting man I would stake all my money on it. The divers who found these four anchors within a few yards of each other found them in exactly the location described by the Bible 2,000 years ago!

The evidence is overwhelmingly! Read Acts 27 and you will see what I mean. It's interesting that an entire chapter in the book of Acts would give so much detail as to the location of Paul's shipwreck!

#1 They verifiably date to the 1ˢᵗ century shipping era when Paul's shipwreck occurred
#2 They were found on the only shoreline that Paul's ship could have approached under those conditions: the southeast shoreline
#3 There were found on a reef just near the entrance of the bay
#4 They were found in the exact 90 feet of water that was recorded by the sailors on Paul's ship
#5 All four were found within a 40-yard radius
#6 There were found near a sandy beach, which is unusual for Malta.
#7 They were found in a location that Paul's sailors, and all sailors at that time, would have been unfamiliar with.
#8 They were found in a place where two seas meet under stormy conditions

There is no other location around Malta that comes close to fitting all of these Biblical clues. We may have touched and handled the only true Biblical relic that still exists today from New Testament times!

Today the anchor stocks are on display in the Malta museum.

Bob and I at a historic temple site on Malta dating back to the B.C. era

Two years earlier I had gone on another adventure with Bob and several friends. This trip was to the country of Iran, doing research on Noah's ark. Our team, headed by Bob Cornuke, included John Tomlin, a friend of mine who lost his son in the Columbine tragedy, Larry Williams, father of the movie star, Michelle Williams, Todd Phillips, a youth pastor from Austin, Texas, Dick Bright, a seasoned ark hunter, Paul Cornuke, Bob's brother, David Holbrook, author, Dan Toth, an ex-navy SEAL, and me.

The 8 of us would spend the next 2 weeks in the rugged mountains of Iran, staying in nomad camps and in tents.

Our team under a very unfriendly sign in Tehran!

We had so many adventures and memories that I can't possibly cover, but I will share 2 of those. We faced real danger while we were there - - danger that was potentially life threatening in one village.

The remote villages that we entered looked like movie sets from centuries ago. As we entered one of the villages, the first sight that met our eyes was a goat with its throat slit, hanging from a tripod made of tree limbs and blood running down into a small stream.

One of the Iranian mountain villages we went through

In one of the villages, we learned that there was a large swimming pool stone-type structure in the middle of town where all the men would gather at noon and splash around in to cool off. We went to that location and there were around 50 Muslim men in the pool singing.

We decided to join them, so we stripped down to our underpants and got in with them. At first, they all kept their distance from us, but as we smiled and showed friendly faces, they slowly warmed up to us.

One of the guys in our group suggested that since they were singing, we should counter with our own song. The 8 of us began singing "Amazing Grace". A stillness fell over their entire group and you could feel God's presence resting on all of us - - Christian and Muslim. When we finished singing there was silence.

Then they began to clap and came over with high fives and pats on our backs. It was an experience I will never forget.

We stayed in tents in a massive valley high in the mountains of Iran for several nights. There was no food available except what we purchased from local shepherds - - and that was fresh lamb. No fruit, no vegetables - - just lamb, for over a week!

Each evening after we were finished hiking and exploring, the shepherds would bring a lamb into camp and we would watch as they slit its throat and bled it out, then cut up the meat for our meal.

I was talking to Larry Williams about how Rachel's name meant "little lamb" in Hebrew, and I shared with him how Jesus was called the lamb of God and was led to Calvary like a lamb to the slaughter.

Larry Williams and Darrell in Iran

Sitting by the fire that night I turned to Bob and said, *"Bob, I don't know what they call this place, but I am renaming it, "Rachel's Valley"*. Tear came into his eyes, and he said, *"I will always remember this place as exactly that, "Rachel's Valley."*

204

I wish I could tell you that we found Noah's ark on that venture, but we didn't. However, we found a lot of clues that would lead to Bob's next trip to Iran and the discovery that might well be the ark of Noah. I was not able to go on that next trip, but my good friend Josh McDowell was with Bob when they found a massive structure of petrified wood on a mountain peak, surrounded by signs of sea life. Numerous seashells were there.

A piece of petrified wood from the ark-like structure that Bob discovered on his final visit to Iran

To read more about their discovery, go to Bob's website at www.baseinstitute.org or Google "Base Institute".

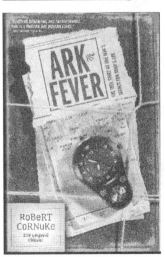

Bob's book, "Ark Fever" tells the story of incredible adventures, beginning with he astronaut, Jim Irwin, searching all over Mt. Ararat and coming to the conclusion that it was the wrong mountain.

This is an amazing book that will keep you on the edge of your seat, and describes, in much more detail, the trip that I was privileged to go on with Bob and our incredible team of adventurers.

205

Chapter 21

RACHEL'S ACCOLADES & AWARDS

As Rachel's story began to be heard throughout the United States, as well as in other countries, she would be recognized with accolades and awards.

One of the first awards came from the Acts of Kindness Association which posthumously awarded her the National Acts of Kindness Award as Student of the Year in 2001.

We met with and received letters from 3 Presidents of the United States who heard segments of Rachel's story.

THE WHITE HOUSE

WASHINGTON

May 13, 1999

Mr. Darrell Scott
3087 East Fall Lane
Littleton, Colorado   80126

Dear Mr. Scott:

Hillary and I were deeply saddened about your daughter's death. We know our words cannot ease the pain you are feeling, but we wanted you to know that you are in our thoughts and prayers. We know how dearly you loved Rachel and understand, if only in our worst fears, the horror of what has happened in your lives.

All Americans share your grief. Such senseless violence and hatred hurt each of us, though few have had to endure its effects as personally as you have. We pray that God's grace will sustain you during this terrible time and that the loving support of your family, friends, and the entire Littleton community will bring you comfort and strength in the days ahead.

Sincerely,

Bill Clinton

This one was sent to us from President Clinton less than a month after Rachel died.

No amount of sympathy could possibly stem the flow of grief that we were experiencing during those days, but we were grateful for the outpouring of love and support, letters, and cards from so many.

207

Darrell, President Clinton, & Craig in the Oval Office

Sandy, President Clinton, & Darrell in Colorado

As *Rachel's Challenge* went into more and more schools, we began to receive accolades from all over the nation. There were so many that I can't possibly show pictures of them all.

This was a letter sent to us from President George W. Bush after he began to her about *Rachel's Challenge* and our influence in American schools.

THE WHITE HOUSE

WASHINGTON

September 20, 2002

I send greetings to those gathered to participate in Rachel's Challenge.

Our Nation needs Americans who respond to the call to serve others, stand up for the weak, and sacrifice for a greater good. Through the gathering momentum of millions of acts of kindness and decency, we will change America one soul at a time and build a culture of service, citizenship, and respect. By pledging to help their neighbor, young people help to strengthen our Nation and inspire others in their community to do the same.

I commend Rachel's Challenge for encouraging our youth to make a difference in our schools and neighborhoods. I also ask that students continue to set high goals and work hard to achieve them.

Laura joins me in sending our best wishes.

George Bush

Craig Scott & President Bush share a speaking event

Craig, Laura Bush, Sandy, & Darrell

We received this letter from President Trump after I was asked to speak at the White house concerning school safety, following the terrible school shooting in Parkland, Florida in which 17 people were killed and 17 others wounded.

THE WHITE HOUSE

WASHINGTON

March 12, 2018

Mr. and Mrs. Darrell Scott
Lone Tree, Colorado

Dear Sandra and Darrell:

I am grateful you were able to join us at the White House for a listening session regarding school safety.

Our entire Nation continues to mourn the innocent lives taken from us by every horrific act of evil that has occurred in our schools. We hold the memory of your daughter, Rachel, and every child we have tragically lost, in our hearts.

The strength you have demonstrated in the years since Rachel's passing has touched people all across our Nation. I appreciate the meaningful work you continue to do with Rachel's Challenge. As you said, we must work together to create a culture in our country that encourages deep and meaningful connections with one another.

Thank you again for being with us. May God bless you.

Sincerely,

Meeting at Trump Tower

Her story would be told or referred to in over 40 books by different authors just in the first 5 years following the tragedy. Numerous magazines featured articles about her like the one from Teen People Magazine:

In 2006, on behalf of Rachel and *Rachel's Challenge*, I was awarded the "Friend of Education" award by the National Education Association of New York.

In 2009 I was selected by Major League Baseball and People Magazine to represent the Colorado Rockies at the All-Star Game in St. Louis, Missouri.

Each major league baseball team had one representative from a non-profit organization chosen to represent their home team. I was fortunate to be able to represent my daughter and our organization, *Rachel's Challenge* at the event.

I even got to participate in announcing some plays from the broadcast booth during a Colorado Rockies game.

215

It was an event that Sandy and I enjoyed, and I wish so much that Rachel could see how she would be honored there.

This is the award that they sent from MLB and People Magazine.

In 2010 the Friends of Texas Public Schools awarded Sandy and I the Texas education "Friend of the Year" award on behalf of *Rachel's Challenge*.

Our friends, Chuck and Gena Norris were with us at this event, and the very next year they received the same award for their organization, KickstartKids.

We have been in so many schools in the state of Texas throughout the years and continue to do so. One of our speakers, Cody Hodges, was the quarterback at Texas Tech years ago, and he went to many of the schools in the Texas "panhandle" year after year.

I spoke to a prestigious group of city leaders from the Dallas area in the VIP lounge at the Texas Rangers facility several years ago. A representative from Belo television corporation was there and when they heard Rachel's story the executive team contacted us and asked to partner with us around the nation.

They owned primary tv stations in over 20 city markets such as: WFAA NBC Dallas, KHOU CBS Houston, KING NBC Seattle, KMOV CBS St. Louis, KTVK Phoenix, NBC KGWTV NBC Portland, KTVB Boise, and over a dozen more.

I went to every single one of their stations throughout an entire year and presented to all of their staff and employees and they gave us exposure nationwide to millions of viewers. Because of their involvement with Rachel's Challenge, Belo was awarded the National Community Service Award.

National Community Service Award to Belo TV Corporation for partnering with Rachel's Challenge

The city leaders in San Diego come together for an annual awards banquet. *Rachel's Challenge* received the Community Conflict Prevention Award. Rob Unger, our CEO at that time, and Fred Lynch, one of our presenters, were there with us.

Dick Enberg was the host of the banquet. He and I had a long talk backstage. He passed away just a short time after this event. Hall of Fame basketball player, Bill Walton, and his wife, introduced Sandy and I to the crowd before we received the award.

Sandy receiving the San Diego Award

Documentaries on Rachel's life won three Emmy Awards in three different cities: Seattle, Phoenix, and Atlanta.

In December, 2018, Time Magazine did a story about parents who had lost their children to violence. We were all chosen because we each were pursuing solutions, in our own way, to the violence in our schools. Of course, my contribution was Rachel's story and *Rachel's Challenge*. Each of the other parents had powerful stories to share.

Sandy and I were awarded the keys to several cities around the United States by mayors who were impacted by Rachel's story.

I spoke at Police Academies, police staffs, and prisons numerous times and was given quite a few honorary police badges.

James Burton (Elvis's guitar player)

Dr. Oz donated promos for Rachel's Challenge

Randy Travis

Sawyer Brown - - Mark Miller (red cap) & Hobie

Oak Ridge Boys (Paul Jackson on the right)

Governor of South Dakota: Kristi Noem

Former Colorado Governor Owens & Mrs. Owens

Former Ohio Governor Taft with Dana and Darrell

Former Colorado Governor Ritter

LAS VEGAS CITY LEADERS

Bill Ripken (Former MLB Player & MLB Announcer)

Tony Romo: Former Dallas Cowboys Quarterback

Chris Collinsworth
(Former NFL Player & NFL Announcer)

NFL Hall of Famer Tony Dorsett

Gabriel Landeskog: Captain of Colorado Avalanche

Brian Griese & Dr. Brook Griese

With Lombardi Super Bowl Trophy

Darrell Speaking to Indianapolis Colts Staff

Shane Hamman: Olympic Weightlifter and World Record Holder - - Shane was a Speaker for Rachel's Challenge for several years

Loren Cunningham: Founder of Youth With A Mission

Josh McDowell

**David Barton & Darrell
with Original Revolutionary War Muskets**

**MARY LOU RETTON
OLYMPIC CHAMPION GYMNAST**

**GOOSE GOSSAGE: HALL OF FAME
BASEBALL PITCHER FOR NY YANKEES**

**CHRISTIAN MOORE: FOUNDER OF WHYTRY
& ONE OF MY CLOSEST FRIENDS**

**DR. ROBERT MARZANO (L) FOUNDER OF MARZANO
RESEARCH & DR. JIM FAY: FOUNDER OF LOVE &
LOGIC   2 VERY DEAR FRIENDS!**

In 2011 I was asked to go to Charlotte, North Carolina to speak to the mayor and city leaders. I was invited to speak at the NASCAR Hall of Fame where some of the most famous race cars in NASCAR history are on display.

Chapter 22
MEDIA MANIA

The first few years after the tragedy at Columbine the media continued to produce specials, documentaries, and interviews about it. As I began to speak around America, the national media was constantly appearing at the events. There is almost always local news stations at our events, but the first couple of years it was local *and* national.

The media gave us an opportunity to let more people know about Rachel's story and the great work being done by *Rachel's Challenge*. Here are just a few of the many pictures from interviews that we did over the years:

I still get calls from the national media from time to time to comment on issues like gun control, school shootings, or *Rachel's Challenge.*

We have been blessed to partner with many local tv stations around the nation that have helped promote *Rachel's Challenge* in their schools. Atlanta, Boise, Seattle, Denver, Dallas, and many more.

Chapter 23
FAMILY, FRIENDS, EMPLOYEES, AND ROAD WARRIORS

Sandy and I are so grateful for our eight children and 13 grandchildren (*with more to come*). This is just a quick update, while this book is being written on where everyone is and what they are doing. All of them live in the Denver area except Craig, who lives in Atlanta, and our grandson, Arthur who lives in Germany.

Rachel's oldest sister, Bethanee, is married to Don McCandless, who is a Project Manager for a commercial construction company. Bethanee is an educational assistant at an elementary school and loves working with little children.

She and Don have 2 children, Brandon, who just recently graduated from high school, and Cheyenne, who is still in school.

Dana, Rachel's next oldest sister, is married to John Bollwerk, who is a Facility Maintenance Manager, and is on the board of the Hanson Research Station that is a dinosaur dig that has uncovered many dinosaur skeletons. Dana is a stay-at-home mom who is home schooling their three children, Jason, Claire, and Veronica.

Craig, Rachel's younger brother, lives in Atlanta where he works in the movie industry and speaks in schools with his own program. Craig was a speaker for *Rachel's Challenge* for several years. Craig has had an opportunity to work with some of the biggest names in the film industry.

Mike, Rachel's youngest brother, has been a valuable part of *Rachel's Challenge* for many years. He wears several hats at our office, from content development, to project management, to product delivery. Mike has a son, Arthur, who lives with his mom in Germany.

Rachel would be proud of all her siblings! She also has four stepbrothers who she got to know and love before she died.

Ryan Hollingshead is her oldest stepbrother, and he is a high school principal at a Parker, Colorado high school. He is married to Belinda, who is a real estate agent. They have two children, Noah, who recently graduated from Colorado State University, and AnnMarie, who is still in college.

Cory Hollingshead is a paramedic and firefighter. He is married to Jen, who works part time for *Rachel's Challenge*. They have two daughters, Skylar and Peyton who are both still in school.

Tyler Hollingshead is Senior Director of Application Strategy for Visa. His wife, Jackie, is owner at Dash Imaging, an ultrasound company. They have 3 children. Twins, Colton and Ashley, and their younger sister, Morgan. All three are still in school.

Rachel's mom, Beth Nimmo, is married to Larry Nimmo, who is a Public Works Director for the city of Parker, Colorado. Beth has also shared Rachel's story with many people as well.

Rachel's stepbrother (Larry's son), Matthew, is an EMR Surgeon. His wife, Mimi, is the Healthcare Simulation Educator at Children's Hospital. Matthew and Mimi, have a son, named Henry.

From 2020-2023 I was in and out of hospitals with health issues. I had a quadruple bypass several other surgeries.

Today I am healthy and full of energy again. I continue to develop content for *Rachel's Challenge*. I also continue to travel and speak in conferences, churches, and community events.

Sandy is Vice-President and Social Activities Director.

My brother, Larry, was a speaker for *Rachel's Challenge* for many years. He and his wife, Mary, have two children, Jeff and Sarah, who were both close to Rachel. They also have four grandchildren. Larry now lives in Louisiana and works as a driver for oil field equipment. I love my brother!

Over the last 25 years, we have been honored to make so many new friends. Our *Rachel's Challenge* staff has always felt like family to us. Here is a picture of our team of employees, presenters, and some board members taken in 2012.

There were many who came before this group and many who have come and gone since this picture was taken. Below is some of our presenters taken in 2018.

Rob Unger served as our CEO for 14 years. He became a dear friend and travel companion for many events over those years.

Before joining *Rachel's Challenge*, Rob had a successful 27-year in business, including time with IBM and GE Capital.

Rob's time and contribution to *Rachel's Challenge* will forever be remembered. He helped guide us through many ups and downs on our quest to impact lives.

Kristi Krings took over as CEO after Rob left and has done an amazing job of taking us from the "covid years" back to reaching more and more students.

Kristi was Miss Montana in the 2001 Miss USA pageant. She would later win the John Lennon songwriting competition grand prize and would become a two-time platinum singer/songwriter. She was a speaker for *Rachel's Challenge* for several years before moving to New York to work as a Head of Partnerships for UNiDAYS. She returned back to *Rachel's Challenge* as CEO in 2022.

The covid era caused most schools in America to shut down for a year.

We were used to being in hundreds of schools each year and in 2021 we were only in eight schools! Kristi worked hard to help revive the organization and put it back on track. Sandy and I just love this lady and her husband, Aric.

Andrew Strait took over our sales manager's position after our former sales manager left to start his own company. Andrew has become one of my closest friends and has traveled with me all over the country. Andrew left Rachel's Challenge in 2022 but remains a dear friend.

Dr. Robert Marzano is one of the gurus of educational research for K-12 schools in America. He has written dozens of books, including two that I helped co-author with him. He and I traveled together all over the country doing conferences. He and his wife, Jana, are some of our dearest friends.

2024 DENVER BASED STAFF

In the above picture is my youngest son, Mike Scott, on the far left side. Mike is the Product and Ecommerce Manager.

Sandy and I are standing next to Mike. Sandy is the co-founder and Vice President of Rachel's Challenge.

Patrick Nixon, standing behind the tv, is the Senior Manager of Operations and Travel Coordinator for our speakers.

Peter DeAnello is on the tv on the left and is a Regional Partnership Manager.

Sage Robinson (tv on the right) is a Regional Partnership Manager.

JoAnne Allen (by right side of tv) is an Accountant.

Denise Chavez (middle front right) is the Account Manager and has been with Rachel's Challenge longer than any other employee.

Kelly Campman is the KC/FOR Club Director and HR Manager.

In the earliest years my friend, Wayne Worthy traveled with me and helped manage the early years of Rachel's Challenge. Wayne and I have been best friends for almost 50 years. He and his wife, Betsy, knew Rachel from the time she was a baby.

WAYNE WORTHY  **DARRELL SCOTT**

Peter DeAnello and Sage Robinson, two of our sales representatives, are also close friends and have flown around the states with me, experiencing the rental car, hotel, fast food circuit that all speakers live with.

Peter DeAnello & Darrell **Sage Robinson**

Peter and I are standing at the spot where Rachel died. This spot was outside the school at the time she was murdered.

Bryan Boorujy, another very close friend, was our videographer for many years and traveled with me, not only to many states, but also to Bermuda and Malta.

Bob Mumford has been a "pappa" to me ever since my teen years. He has been an anchor in my life through all the ups and downs throughout the years with my health and with *Rachel's Challenge*. Sandy and I love Bob and his wife, Judith.

We are so grateful for all the *Rachel's Challenge* employees, current and past: Denise Chavez, JoAnne Allen, Kelly Campman, Patrick Nixon, Sarah Branion, Andrew Cippola, Mike Scott, Jeremy Kreft, Karissa McCoy, Jen Hollingshead, Belinda Hollingshead, Dana Bollwerk, Nancy Boorujy, John Corcoran, Tom Isaacson, Keren Kilgore, Vicki Leroue, Tawny McVay, Tristan Mraz, Lindsey Reese, John Richmond, Jessica Sneiders, Michelle Smith, Janet Stumbo, Bryan Van Welzen, Lauren Zerbst, Jennifer Zurek, and I have to stop, because I am getting old and can't remember everyone's name that were employed by *Rachel's Challenge.*

There were also a number of part-time employees through the years. If you are reading this and you worked as an employee for Rachel's Challenge, and I did not include your name, please forgive me and know that you are appreciated!

The list of presenters is just too long for my memory, but you are the true road warriors who helped carry this message to millions of students around the world. Thank you, thank you, thank you!

Over the years we lost three of our beloved team members who have passed on, and I want to acknowledge them:

Zach Lucero worked in our shipping department in the early days of *Rachel's Challenge.* He had been a gang member and had run ins with the law, but found a home with *Rachel's Challenge*, where he was loved and accepted. Zach was a very hard worker and we miss him.

Tim Sanderford helped bring me into my original home state of Louisiana for speaking engagements. Tim and I became close friends long before he became an employee of *Rachel's Challenge.*

We hired Tim as our product shipping manager and everyone in the office just loved him.

250

He always had a joke and a smile on his lips and at times his outrageous humor had us all in stitches. He passed away shortly before the covid pandemic hit, and we miss him very much.

TIM SANDERFORD

Jim May had been a close friend of mine for many years before Rachel died. He and I spent hours and hours talking about different subjects that would probably bore other people to death. I loved Jim like a brother. His wife, Renee, is a sweet lady. Sandy and I still try to get together with her for lunch whenever we can. Jim was a speaker for *Rachel's Challenge*, but he also brought an element of fun and laughter to the whole staff. Jim, we love you and miss you!

Below is a picture taken at our 2018 speaker training session.

OUR SPEAKERS BACK IN 2018

Chapter 24
FINAL PICTURES AND THOUGHTS

There is so much more that could be written about the impact Rachel's life has had on millions of people's hearts, but we will end with an assortment of pictures from her life.

With Grandpa and Grandma Scott

Dana holding Rachel   **With siblings & cousins**

256

257

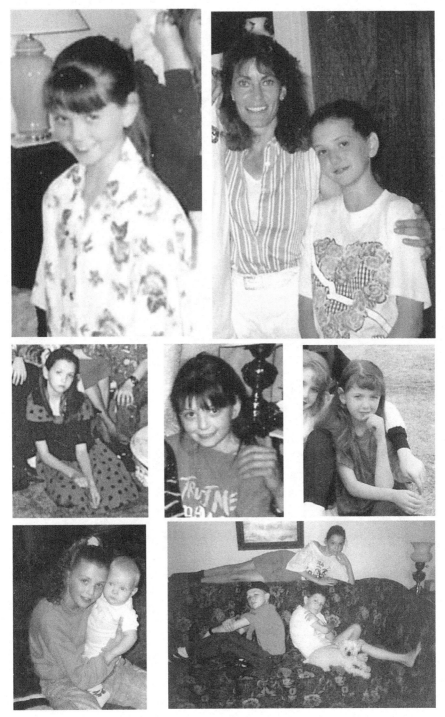

Stepbrother Ryan, Bethanee, Craig, Dana, Rachel, Mike

262

We started this book talking about all the roses that Rachel drew. It seems ironic that the last picture ever taken of her would be with her wearing a rose. It was a picture taken at her high school prom, just days before she would be killed.

There is so much more to Rachel's story that this book could not contain, and we encourage you to go online and watch different videos about her and about *Rachel's Challenge.*

To have Darrell Scott come and speak to your church, business, or community group, contact: Dana at: gocardinals2009@gmail.com or Peter at: peterdeanello@mac.com

To see Darrell's vlogs and video poems go to YouTube: Awareness by Darrell Scott

Darrell Scott has authored over 15 books.
To see more of Darrell's books go to Amazon.

Final Acknowledgements

Special thanks to Wes Yoder, Dana Ashley, Gene Bedley, Joe Coles, Neila Conners, Jeanette Phillps, Gene Burton, Paul and Vicki LeRoue, Virdie Montgomery, Robert Marzano, Jeff Jones, and many others who have contributed to Rachel's legacy.